D1262092

# The Good Corporate Citizen

## A Practical Guide

DORIS RUBENSTEIN

WILEY

John Wiley & Sons, Inc.

658.408
R89g

This book is printed on acid-free paper. ∞

Copyright © 2004 by John Wiley & Sons, Inc. All rights reserved.

Published by John Wiley & Sons, Inc., Hoboken, New Jersey
Published simultaneously in Canada

No part of this publication may be reproduced, stored in a retrieval
system, or transmitted in any form or by any means, electronic,
mechanical, photocopying, recording, scanning, or otherwise, except
as permitted under Section 107 or 108 of the 1976 United States
Copyright Act, without either the prior written permission of the
Publisher, or authorization through payment of the appropriate per-copy
fee to the Copyright Clearance Center, Inc., 222 Rosewood Drive,
Danvers, MA 01923, (978) 750-8400, fax (978) 750-4470, or on the web
at *www.copyright.com*. Requests to the Publisher for permission should
be addressed to the Permissions Department, John Wiley & Sons, Inc.,
111 River Street, Hoboken, NJ 07030, 201-748-6011, fax 201-748-6008,
e-mail: permcoordinator@wiley.com.

Limit of Liability/Disclaimer of Warranty: While the publisher and
author have used their best efforts in preparing this book, they make no
representations or warranties with respect to the accuracy or completeness
of the contents of this book and specifically disclaim any implied
warranties of merchantability or fitness for a particular purpose. No
warranty may be created or extended by sales representatives or written
sales materials. The advice and strategies contained herein may not
be suitable for your situation. You should consult with a professional
where appropriate. Neither the publisher nor author shall be liable
for any loss of profit or any other commercial damages, including but
not limited to special, incidental, consequential, or other damages.

For general information on our other products and services, or
technical support, please contact our Customer Care Department
within the United States at 800-762-2974, outside the United
States at 317-572-3993 or fax 317-572-4002.

Wiley also publishes its books in a variety of electronic formats.
Some content that appears in print may not be available in
electronic books.

For more information about Wiley products, visit our web site
at *www.wiley.com*.

ISBN: 0-471-47565-3

Printed in the United States of America

MIC    10 9 8 7 6 5 4 3 2 1

*To the teachers who taught and encouraged me to write.*

University Libraries
Carnegie Mellon University
Pittsburgh PA 15213-3890

# Contents

# Foreword

Doris Rubenstein has written an important book because the topic she presents falls into an uncomfortable gray area of social and economic conviction. We like certainty; with set parameters we can order our lives more convincingly. But what of the purpose of a business: where is certainty there?

Are business operations to be solely focused, laser-like, on profit for the business owners, at all costs? If they are not, what then is their purpose—or, to acknowledge the complexity of the matter, their purposes?

Should business stand in for government and seek to provide public goods because to do so, especially when governments lack revenue or administrative capacity, would be nice and helpful?

Should business stand in for charities because business has money? The logic here is the moral intuition that "can" should give rise to "ought." When we have the power to make a difference, we should feel some moral suasion to do so. But make a difference for whom? Is business rightly empowered to choose between deserving and undeserving citizens for the conferring of benefits and advantages or the removal of disadvantages?

I think most would agree that business must pay taxes and obey the laws of the land. Most would also agree that business should be about making a profit and not wasting capital or effort on subsidizing losses. These are the two extremes of clarity about the role of business in our lives. On the one hand, business contributes to social well-being through obedience to government; on the other hand, it contributes to society by taking care of itself.

Then there is the middle realm: business incurring expenses that detract from net profits (at least in the short run) and that have some public or social appeal as their motivation, such as charitable contributions to the poor. Here is where we find shades of gray and here is where Doris Rubenstein shines her thoughtful analytical light.

Being precise as to the content of business citizenship dispels uncertainty and encourages action. The case to be made for business to assume citizenship duties is an indirect one. I think it arises from the dependence of business on society for vital capital inputs. It is notoriously hard for business to succeed in conditions of war, civil upheaval, or pervasive corruption of public authority, and in cultures of deep mistrust. To be successful for its owners, a business needs to live under the right conditions. Like a plant or any other living organism, business responds to its environment. If nourishment is plentiful and predators few, life will thrive. Animals lack the moral sense and the intelligence to actively improve their environments. That is not true for human animals. We have both a moral sense and intelligence, and we act all the time to improve our condition. We are in a cause-and-effect cycle with our environment because our actions can change our environment, which then changes the inputs we draw on to live.

To my mind, a business is only an extension of the individual. A corporation, for example, aggregates the interests of many individuals and mobilizes individual talents and energies for larger-scale undertakings. Every business, therefore, has the opportunity to provide for its future by improving its environment.

A sensible way for businesses to act constructively is to support government in its proper role. That is cost-effective and provides for public goods. The rule of law is sustained, contracts are enforced, civil society integrates interests and value perspectives into the peaceful evolution of the political order, education and public health are attended to, and levels of trust increase.

But government cannot do everything. In fact, given its bureaucratic nature and perceived need to respond to the fickle winds of political whim, the scope of government's good offices is limited. Many efforts at improving our social and cultural environments are best attempted through the entrepreneurial efforts of civil society—but these efforts must be funded. The organizations that undertake these efforts have no power to tax, nor should they. They must rely for resources on the willing support of citizens, including businesses.

Thus, indirectly helping itself, business through its charitable activities raises the level of what civil society can accomplish, which then changes and improves the environment in which business seeks to make a living.

The calculus by which business can measure the advantages of citizenship is not the normal market calculus of profit and loss on sales. The environmental factors supporting business are not easily converted into prices, and many of them are not for sale; rather, they are sunk-cost capital infrastructures like an educational system. The proper calculus for a business to use is fidelity to a set of principles, such as the Caux Round Table Principles for Business. Qualitative goals have to be set for an environment that sustains capital investment, rewards entrepreneurs, and promotes an educated and loyal workforce. Business can then determine how to improve the conditions on which it relies for long-term profitability.

In this book, Doris Rubenstein gives us a vision of those qualitative goals, along with very practical suggestions for furthering enlightened business self-interest.

STEPHEN B. YOUNG
Global Executive Director
The Caux Round Table

# Preface

I've never worked for a large corporation. Which means to say I've never been on a corporation's payroll. So, then, what qualifies me to be writing this book?

For more than 25 years, I was a fundraiser. Although I didn't work for big business, I worked with corporate America. Working with thoughtful, dedicated corporate staff members, I helped them to achieve their company's mission and philanthropic goals as they related to the organizations I represented. This gave me many opportunities to see the planning and execution of a variety of good corporate citizenship programs.

Over the years, I took notes and kept files of materials on the best that I encountered. When I started consulting on corporate citizenship, these examples became the basis of my program, which is described in this book for you.

The purpose of this book is to take you step-by-step through a process that reflects the best practices in corporate citizenship—and particularly corporate philanthropy—used by many of our country's top businesses. I ask questions and offer suggestions, options, and some answers to help you consider and recognize what choices are out there for your own company when developing your own corporate citizenship program plan.

After providing you with some background and research data on the state of corporate philanthropy in America, *The Good Corporate Citizen: A Practical Guide* gives you much of the help you'll need to create your own plan. The checklists ensure that you're covering all the bases within any given field. There are examples and case studies to help you see how these policies and procedures play out in real life.

Who will find this book useful? In my experience as a consultant, the people I work with most often are CEOs, presidents, Chief Financial Officers, marketing directors, human resources directors, community relations officers, and particularly the special assistants to any of the above. You are in the group I usually find sitting around the table when I conduct my planning workshops.

Fundraisers will also find this book interesting because it allows a peek into the mind of the person who holds the purse strings to that grant you are seeking. It challenges fundraisers to meet the high standards set in the good program that will result from a company's following the process described in this book.

Educators in business know that this subject is not covered in the standard curriculum. It might be mentioned in an ethics class, but the discussion is often theoretical. This book is exactly what the title says it is: a practical guide. Using each chapter in Part Two as a point of departure, you can develop a lesson plan for the better part of a semester that will leave your students fully prepared to competently address these situations when they encounter them in their future business lives.

Finally, any individual who is interested in upgrading his or her charitable giving from arbitrary to philanthropic, and finally to magnanimous, will do well to read and consider the lessons here. Much of what is presented can easily be adapted for personal giving and family foundations.

What you will not find in this book is a cookie-cutter model for your company to use, or a template that you can use to fill in the blanks and—voilá—have a quality program. This guide provides you with questions to answer and choices to make, according to what is best for your own situation.

It is not completely comprehensive. If it were, this would not be just one book, but a volume on each of the chapters in Part Two. If you use it well, you will still be pleased with your product, especially after working the minor bugs out over the course of the first year of your program.

Most of the examples are drawn from the economic life of the Minneapolis–St. Paul area, where I have lived for the past 20 years. This community has been known nationally for its high level of corporate philanthropy for many years, so I believe that these examples are good ones for others to follow.

# Acknowledgments

When it comes to acknowledgments, I first ask you to join me in giving sincere thanks to the contributions officers—whatever their real job titles were—at the many outstanding businesses I worked with as a fundraiser: Frank Reed at IBM, Lew Alpaugh at the old American Hoechst, Reatha Clark King at the General Mills Foundation, Kay O'Keefe at the Medtronic Foundation, Gregg McPherson and Tony Yapel at 3M, and many more. Their thoughtful, ethical grant-making informs this book and made the organizations and projects they funded better in many, many ways.

My brother-in-law, Dr. Marvin Cohen, offered wonderful advice on the use of a variety of graphics to demonstrate numerous practical and didactic points. Emily Swanson assisted in formatting the text. Good luck in your new career in education, Emily! Paige Catherine Rubenstein was a constant, patient companion. Her unquestioning devotion and her good humor made life easier when I felt isolated after long days on the word processor.

Lastly, thanks to my editor, Susan McDermott, for her guidance, patience, skill, faith, and enthusiasm in championing a first-time author.

# PART ONE

# Background

## CHAPTER 1

# Philanthropy and Corporate Citizenship

President Calvin Coolidge stated that "The business of America is business." The truth of that statement has been debated on various levels ever since it was made. What follows is the question, "What is the purpose of business?"

Depending on your point of view, the answer can be either "To improve the conditions of the entrepreneur and the investor who created the business" or "To improve the condition of society in general." Some argue that the latter will flow from the former. Others point out that raising the general condition of society creates an atmosphere that will be better for business in the long run.

It is the rare business owner who doesn't recognize the value of meeting social responsibilities by making donations or contributing volunteer time. Charles Dickens knew that his readers would find it amusing for Scrooge to reply, "Let them die, then, and decrease the surplus population," to his associates who asked him for alms for the poor at Christmastime. Victorian England knew that charity is a part of good citizenship. Today's Americans know it just as well.

Why conduct a corporate citizenship program? Simply put, it's good for business. According to Brian O'Connell, in his 1999 book *Civil Society: The Under-pinnings of American Democracy,*[1] companies that received the Ad Council's Public Service Award showed annual growth in profits of 11 percent compounded over 30 years. That is three times better than the growth of the Gross National Product during the same period!

Michael E. Porter, a Harvard professor, and Mark R. Kramer, a business consultant and cofounder of the Center for Effective Philanthropy, present compelling evidence that proves the effectiveness of good corporate citizenship in "The Competitive Advantage of Corporate Philanthropy."[2] In this report, published in the *Harvard Business Review,* the authors stress the importance of strategic philanthropy in creating value in the act and process of giving. Through strategic philanthropy, a company can influence what Porter and Kramer call the "competitive context" of its home and market communities.

## COMPETITIVE CONTEXT

Four elements compose what Porter and Kramer call the *competitive context* for business:

1. *Available inputs of production:* employees, material resources, infrastructure for delivery (such as roads, electricity, etc.), tax structure, and so on.

2. *Demand for your company's products or services:* a healthy economy that can consume them.

3. *Healthy competition:* to assure that there is continuous improvement and innovation.

4. *Related and supporting industries:* from parts suppliers to office suppliers.

Giving to improve the competitive context is what creates the value that translates into improved profits. Your ability to compete depends heavily on the competitive context of each location where you do business.

Beyond the competitive context, having a product or service that fills a need at a reasonable price is key. The product or service functions within the competitive context.

### Affecting Your Competitive Context

There are many ways of affecting competitive context. The tax environment is one available input of production. Our many chambers of commerce lobby hard at the legislature level to create a tax code that is favorable to business. This is an exceptionally long process for effecting change. The results are measurable in terms of legislative sessions or executive terms.

In terms of creating demand and participating in healthy competition, billions are spent on advertising in our economy. Whether your company places advertising in the mass media or in trade publications and shows, this is an expensive proposition.

What produces better results? The Harvard report concludes that "[p]hilanthropy can often be the most *cost-effective way* for a company to improve its competitive context, enabling companies to leverage the efforts and infrastructure of nonprofits and other institutions."[3]

Porter and Kramer pinpoint three distinct advantages that business earns by using philanthropy to affect competitive context:

1. *They can use the existing programs and networks of nonprofits and educational institutions.* Supporting nonprofit housing programs in inner cities helps to provide a workforce for downtown industries, such as hotels and restaurants, that have need of unskilled workers. Commercial banks and law firms support organizations such as Habitat for Humanity not because *they* particularly need low-skill workers, but because *their business clients do!*

2. *They can leverage the collective actions of other companies that donate to nonprofits, enabling costs to be spread over multiple donor businesses.* Capital campaigns—from giants like

those at major public and private research universities to build new, state-of-the-art facilities, to small ones like the efforts of a fledgling private elementary school to purchase an inner-city landmark building for expansion—demonstrate the power of cooperation. Although the sign over the main entryway may bear the name of a beloved and respected member of the faculty, the plaques on the interior classrooms and auditoriums tell the real story of dozens of enlightened companies that pulled together to erect the infrastructure of tomorrow's corporate community.

3. *They can forge partnerships among cooperating companies and nonprofits or government units.* This is likely to happen because it removes the appearance of favoritism for one particular company on the part of the charity. In almost any well-designed project for nonprofit enterprise, the costs will be shared among multiple donors, and often with governmental or quasi-governmental units, in *public-private nonprofit partnerships.*

## STRATEGIC PHILANTHROPY

The Harvard report stresses the importance of strategic philanthropy to maximize the effectiveness of efforts to affect the competitive context. Porter and Kramer recommend several points to include in a strategic plan: selecting the best grantees, signaling other funders, improving performance of grantees, and advancing knowledge and practice. Companies developing these plans must weigh the benefits of concentrating their energies on any of these points.

Where most companies go wrong in planning, Porter and Kramer say, is in placing too much money and emphasis strictly on the public relations benefit of their contributions. I carry an old cause-related ad from my local newspaper in my portfolio: it certainly cost the advertiser (a public utility company) several times more to produce and print than the amount of the donation made to the charity being promoted. Often the public can see through these self-congratulatory displays, negating the good will that the donation was meant to build in the first place.

A strategic plan for corporate citizenship requires balance between communal obligation, goodwill building, and strategic giving in order to build competitive context. Improving that context, though, is the best long-term strategy to build long-term profits for business.

## UNDERSTANDING THE PHILANTHROPIC ROOTS OF CORPORATE CITIZENSHIP

Corporate citizenship goes far beyond philanthropy. Good citizenship includes things that are mandated or just good sense: paying taxes equitably and on time; providing fair benefits to employees, providing a safe and healthy workplace, and so on.

To understand corporate philanthropy, let's look briefly at the origins of philanthropy itself. Philanthropy has been around ever since humankind evolved beyond tribalism. Philosophers as far back as Aristotle in the time of classical Greece observed that giving money away is easy, but making a difference with such expenditures can be a challenge.

*Magnanimity* is a big word. For most of us, when we really think about it, it means making sacrifices for worthy ends. That sacrifice is usually money.

*Philanthropy* itself is a big word to wrap our minds around. Going back to its Greek roots, it's simply love of our fellow persons. I'm always reminded of the film version of *The Wizard of Oz*. When the Wizard presented the Tinman with the testimonial for his great heart, the Wizard talked about people who were "philan . . . philly . . . phitha . . . good deed doers." The Wizard knew how to get to the "heart" of the subject! Before we talk about corporate philanthropy, let's examine philanthropy in general and how it differs from charity.

## THE EIGHT STEPS ON THE LADDER OF CHARITY

As we just discussed, philanthropy has been around a long time. One of the most quoted thinkers on the subject is the medieval Jewish sage, Rabbi Moses ben Maimon, commonly called Maimonides. Maimonides wanted to help those who would do good to go on to do the best they possibly could. He likened charity to a ladder. At the bottom rung was a level of charity that even Scrooge could reach. The top rung could be reached only by those who stretched not only financially, but also philosophically in their philanthropic climb.

### Step One:  Giving Charity Grudgingly

We can only hope that in 21st-century America, this scenario would not happen, but picture this: You are walking on a downtown street and you are approached by a sad-looking woman with a child in tow. She asks you for spare change so that she can pay for a bus ride to the social services office.

You are skeptical. Is she really going to use the money for the bus, or is she going to head straight over to the liquor store and drink up your hard-earned coins? You look at the child and decide to hand over whatever is jingling in your pocket. "I'm going to stand here and wait until you get on that bus!" you say. You watch her with a scowl on your face until the bus arrives and she boards.

Yes, you gave. But it was not with a great deal of charity in your heart or your pocket.

### Step Two:  Giving Less than You Should, but Giving Cheerfully

Try this exercise: Think about the last check you wrote to a charity that was not your church or your alma mater. Think about the amount of the check. Now double that amount. Would it have hurt you or your lifestyle to write a check for that sum? Now double *that* amount. Hurting yet? Probably not. Keep doubling the amount until you think that it would bite into your weekly grocery budget, or your monthly mortgage payment. Most of us give far less than our true capacity, whether we give grudgingly or cheerfully.

## Step Three:  Giving Directly to the Poor upon Being Asked

In our day and society, we are rarely asked directly for charity by a poor person. But we *are* asked to give indirectly all the time. In fact, most of us, in both our personal and business lives, are *constantly* being asked to help the poor or some other worthy cause.

Professional fundraisers know the statistics: It takes 11 asks to get a first donation from a new prospect. Even with donors who have already given, it takes seven asks to get each additional contribution. They also know that most people will *not* give unless asked.

Business owners get requests from every corner of their operation: employees, customers, suppliers, partners, community organizations. It boggles the mind to think how many times a week the owner of a $30 million business gets asked for contributions. And you will continue to be asked until you give or you say a definite *no* for all time.

## Step Four:  Giving Directly to the Poor without Being Asked

Having taken us this far on the ladder of charity, Maimonides now puts us in a position to look at three different modalities of giving: Reactive, Active, and Inactive.

Step Three demonstrates the Reactive Mode: You are asked to give, and you react by giving. The way in which you are asked can vary tremendously. You may get a phone call (and we all know how irritating it is to get a telemarketer's call right during dinner, or even the Super Bowl!), or a letter in the mail. The explosive growth of the Internet has brought a concomitant explosion in online solicitations, many of which are scams. You can respond cheerfully with a few coins when you see your fellow Rotarian volunteering at the Salvation Army's red kettle at Christmastime. You may give more generously when that same Rotarian comes knocking on your door for the Rotary Scholarship Fund. All this giving is the *reaction* to being asked.

Step Four addresses the Active form of giving: giving without being asked. There are a lot of reasons why people give this way. One great reason is to avoid the necessity of being asked. If you intend to support an organization such as your alma mater anyway, by making an open-ended pledge and asking to be removed from the solicitation list, you can accomplish your dual goals of supporting a good cause and avoiding calls and letters.

The last giving mode is what many call "Inactive." Inactive giving means that you choose *not* to give when asked (Step Three) and do not engage in Active giving (Step Four). But Inactive giving does not necessarily mean that you will not be giving at all.

Inactive givers allow *others* to make their donation decisions for them. Those others are (most often) bureaucrats in the federal, state, and local governments.

When you make a voluntary donation, it is tax deductible. *You* decide where the money will go, and often how it will be used. Inactive givers forfeit that choice. They may be pleased with how some of the tax dollars they pay are distributed: scientific research at universities or the National Institutes of Health, support of the national park system, and so on. But the bitter debates over too many issues, such as defense or the environment, may give others pause about allowing the government to direct their dollars to questionable projects. There's no avoiding taxes, but philanthropy is one way of counterbalancing political decisions that contradict your interests and values.

## Steps Five and Six:  Indirect Giving

In Step Five, indirect giving, the recipient knows who the giver is, but the giver doesn't know the identity of the recipient. On Step Six, the giver knows who the recipient is, but the recipient doesn't know the identity of the giver.

We're now getting more into how modern charities are organized: namely, through nonprofit organizations that mediate between donors and beneficiaries. These two steps assure that the dignity of the beneficiary is maintained. A recipient of charity should not feel that he or she is less of a human being merely because he or she is receiving aid.

Even in situations such as these, there are some benefits to the donors and recipients knowing each other. Let's take the case of a college student who receives a named scholarship donated by your company. Students are thrilled to receive grants and scholarships that they do not need to repay financially. Most students receive their scholarships in one check, along with money from other financial aid sources. They may or may not be aware that some of the money comes from "Your Company's Scholarship Fund." To them, it's all one big financial aid kettle in the sky.

When they have a chance to meet you and others from your company, though, several very positive things can happen:

- It can be the start of a professionally and personally satisfying, long-term relationship that might lead to the student eventually working for your company.

- The student and her network of family and friends get a wonderful insight into your company. This can lead to them becoming new or better customers, or lead to others taking employment with you.

- The student comes to realize that the money didn't come out of some mysterious pool, but rather from real people who chose to make a difference in her life. The light goes on—which shows the student that someday she, too, can be a donor.

In these situations, no one is insulted or humiliated. This can be an enlightening, educational experience for all involved.

## Step Seven: Anonymity

With true anonymity, neither the donor nor the recipient knows the identity of the other. Here's where today's charity stands, for the most part. Unless the recipients look at the organization's annual report list of donors, they have no idea of who is supporting the program that provides aid to them. Yes, the artist is often asked to attend a special reception before or after a museum show or concert with major donors. Seldom, if ever, is a resident of a battered women's shelter asked to meet with donors while she is in crisis.

## Step Eight: Helping a Person to Avoid Needing Charity

Step Eight can be a pre-need step to help persons avoid situations in which they will need help in the first place; or a curative step, giving the persons the means to lift themselves out of the condition requiring charity. Grants to medical research might fall into this category, because the intent is that disabling or life-threatening diseases might be cured or eliminated. Education, job training, and even free or low-interest business loans fall into Step Eight. Self-sufficiency is its defining trait. It is Step Eight that distinguishes charity (making a gift) from philanthropy (making a difference).

Few companies in America are as admired as Johnson & Johnson. The Robert Wood Johnson Foundation is a direct outgrowth of J&J. The foundation concentrates on making grants in health care, a natural focus for a business that deals in that area. Time has already proved the value of the Robert Wood Johnson Foundation's focussed philanthropy. Research from its sponsored scientists has resulted in important breakthroughs in improving health for those who suffer from numerous conditions.

It would be impossible to name all of the companies, which employ millions of workers, that were started as the result of discoveries in American university laboratories, supported by research grants from other companies. Medtronic, one of the world's largest manufacturers of cardiac pacemakers, was founded by an eternally-grateful alumnus of the University of Minnesota, Earl Bakken. Medtronic and its foundation give back in the form of scholarships and research grants. Medtronic will never recapture most of that "social investment" in philanthropy. Earl Bakken is just fine with that situation.

# THE MINNESOTA PRINCIPLES AND THE CAUX ROUND TABLE

In 1981, a group of far-sighted business leaders calling themselves the Minnesota Business Partnership (MBP) organized to address issues relating to corporate citizenship, and in 1992 they took a daring step. (Earl Bakken was not in the MBP, but it's clear he shared their vision.) The MBP developed a set of five propositions, with two purposes in mind:

1. To describe a system of ethics for international trade.
2. To develop a universally acceptable standard of business behavior.

After the organization of the Minnesota Business Partnership, in 1986, an international group of business leaders (with some crossover from the MBP) formed the Caux Round Table. Based in Switzerland, the Caux Round Table's aim is to address the role that business plays in identifying and promoting solutions to problems that stand in the way of advancing a more prosperous, sustainable, and equitable world society.

The Caux Round Table also developed and issued a set of *Principles for Business,* based in part on the Minnesota Principles. The final point on the Caux Round Table agenda calls for a company adhering to these principles to "be a good corporate citizen through charitable donations, educational and cultural contributions, and employee participation in community and civic affairs." They saved the best for last.

## CHAPTER 2

# Why Conduct a Corporate Citizenship Program?

To answer the question in this chapter's title, let's look at some of the information from and conclusions offered in recent research. In 2000, the Conference Board issued *Consumer Expectations on the Social Accountability of Business*,[1] America's Charities published *Employee Workplace Campaigns at the Crossroads*,[2] and the Council on Foundations reported on *Measuring the Business Value of Corporate Philanthropy*.[3] Two facts came through loud and clear in all three reports: Both consumers and employees expect business to actively help build a better society, and both consumers and employees reward those that do.

The reports found that customers favor businesses with good corporate citizenship programs. As a result, they:

- Are likely to continue doing business with the company.
- Are more willing to recommend company offerings.
- Are less susceptible to switching to a different company for a better financial deal.
- Say that they would choose the company again if picking for the first time.

The assumption that a low bid is the end-all in gaining contracts and sales is somewhat of a fallacy. The fact is that 46 percent of those surveyed in the Conference Board report stated that they were strongly influenced in favor of a particular company over others because of its positive social image. In contrast, 49 percent refused to do business with companies that did not meet their respondents' standard of social responsibility (see Exhibit 2.1).

In fact, combining all factors that influence the public's opinion of business, the surveys showed that consumers care more about brand quality and *company image and reputation* than they do about a company's management or business strategy. This is something that

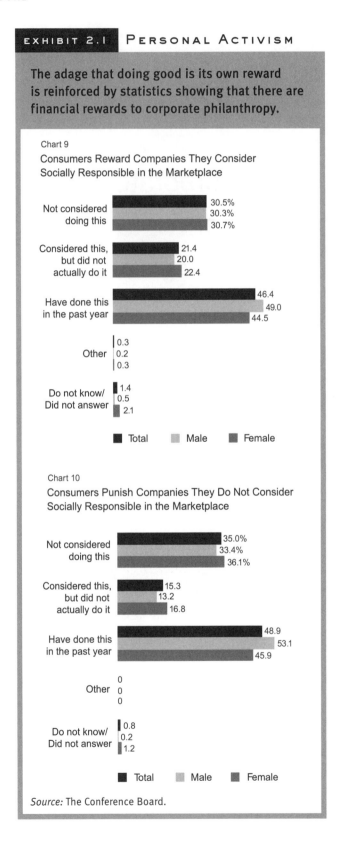

**EXHIBIT 2.1**   PERSONAL ACTIVISM

The adage that doing good is its own reward is reinforced by statistics showing that there are financial rewards to corporate philanthropy.

Chart 9
Consumers Reward Companies They Consider Socially Responsible in the Marketplace

Not considered doing this
30.5%
30.3%
30.7%

Considered this, but did not actually do it
21.4
20.0
22.4

Have done this in the past year
46.4
49.0
44.5

Other
0.3
0.2
0.3

Do not know/ Did not answer
1.4
0.5
2.1

■ Total   ■ Male   ■ Female

Chart 10
Consumers Punish Companies They Do Not Consider Socially Responsible in the Marketplace

Not considered doing this
35.0%
33.4%
36.1%

Considered this, but did not actually do it
15.3
13.2
16.8

Have done this in the past year
48.9
53.1
45.9

Other
0
0
0

Do not know/ Did not answer
0.8
0.2
1.2

■ Total   ■ Male   ■ Female

*Source:* The Conference Board.

company managers *and* company investors should heed carefully, because it is the consumer who ultimately decides a company's success.

## REPUTATION INSURANCE

In the first years of this new century, corporate reputations are falling like bank presidents from skyscraper windows during the 1929 stock market crash. *Fortune 500* firms are being charged with malfeasance and fraud. Investors are selling their shares in these companies en masse. Could management have done anything before the exposé of problems to soften the blow?

They could have made better investments in reputation insurance. Insurance is one of the most costly expenses that businesses incur. They must buy insurance for the health and life of their employees, for liability, for loss, for fire risks, and for innumerable other purposes. These costs can be compounded by negative publicity about corporate behavior—which can lower stock prices for a minimum of six months, according to a study by the University of Southwestern Louisiana.[4] A recent Harris poll shows that businesses with poor corporate citizenship records suffer on the bottom line when customers make choices about purchases and investments.[5]

However, companies with long records of good reputation are less likely to be adversely affected by negative publicity or alleged scandals, according to that Conference Board report.[6] The most important factors in achieving a high rating in reputation was emotional appeal: trust, admiration and respect, and general good feelings.

How is this done? Research conducted by Business for Social Responsibility (*www.bsr.org*) shows that companies with established reputations as good citizens are more likely to be "given a second chance" by stakeholders when problems occur. In other words, good corporate citizenship is a form of reputation insurance.

An outstanding example of the positive effects of corporate philanthropy, as one of the elements in a reputation insurance policy, was the "Tylenol scare" in the 1980s. We have already discussed the reputation that Johnson & Johnson, the manufacturer of Tylenol, has gained through an unparalleled record of support for research and programs in health-related fields. Several deaths occurred after persons ingested tainted Tylenol tablets. J&J admitted no fault in the disaster, but pulled *all*—100 percent—of its Tylenol inventory from the marketplace until it could guarantee that no tainted products would reach consumers. It did the right thing, further bolstering an outstanding reputation built on past performance and philanthropy. As a result, neither J&J's stock price nor its sales were affected.

When electronics retailer Best Buy wanted to move its corporate headquarters into a new community, it sparked a controversy and substantial opposition to the relocation from one property owner, a car dealership with a long residency in the community. Each business claimed to have the best interests of the community at heart. They launched campaigns to demonstrate their commitment to the community. The car dealer, though, despite its decades in the neighborhood, had been only a minor player in civic affairs. Best Buy demonstrated its intentions as a good citizen before the first shovel broke ground on the headquarters building: it instituted a volunteer student mentoring and tutoring program in the middle school, and generously supported popular activities throughout the community. Public opinion was strongly swayed by this largesse, and it gained Best Buy substantial backing from the local residents during a protracted lawsuit brought by the car dealer.

The case of Philip Morris and its Kraft Foods subsidiary is a prime example of investing too late in reputation insurance. Philip Morris is advertising its hunger-relief efforts through Kraft in an attempt to repair the disastrous blows to its reputation from the tobacco trial judgments against the company. Despite this huge campaign, Philip Morris remained at the bottom of the Harris poll list of good corporate reputations. The name Philip Morris became so tarnished that the company recently took a new identity: Altria.

There is no commercial policy available to insure a good reputation. Good corporate citizenship, in the form of a well-developed plan and well-implemented program of product, service, and philanthropy, is the best form of reputation insurance you can get. It's an investment in the company's image, employee morale and loyalty, and the good-will of all its stakeholders.

## Employee Satisfaction and Loyalty

This lesson is particularly important for newer, mid-market businesses that are still building product and service lines, and facing stiff competition from larger, well-established firms that have brand recognition and the advantage in offering a higher level of security and benefits to employees. Employees have come to view corporate citizenship programs as part and parcel of a benefits program. Nearly two-thirds of employees surveyed believe that their companies *should* sponsor a corporate citizenship program of some sort. The reports concur that good corporate citizenship provides benefits to business as employers by improving employee relations in terms of recruitment, morale, loyalty, motivation, and productivity.

Still, the America's Charities report says that there has been a decrease in the percentage of companies with workplace giving programs. What is the reason for this decline? The report points to the growth in medium-size and smaller firms. The real growth in employment is in small, entrepreneurial businesses that lack a history of corporate citizenship, particularly in workplace giving programs like the United Way.

## Other Benefits to Business

Reputation insurance and employee satisfaction are only two reasons to make social investments in the form of philanthropy. Current research shows numerous benefits.

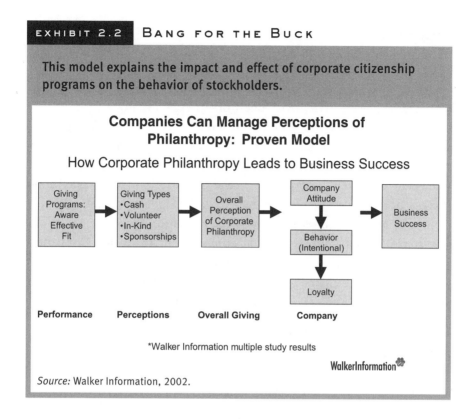

EXHIBIT 2.2    BANG FOR THE BUCK

This model explains the impact and effect of corporate citizenship programs on the behavior of stockholders.

### Companies Can Manage Perceptions of Philanthropy: Proven Model

How Corporate Philanthropy Leads to Business Success

| Giving Programs: Aware Effective Fit | → | Giving Types •Cash •Volunteer •In-Kind •Sponsorships | → | Overall Perception of Corporate Philanthropy | → | Company Attitude ↓ Behavior (Intentional) ↓ Loyalty | → | Business Success |

Performance          Perceptions          Overall Giving          Company

*Walker Information multiple study results

WalkerInformation

Source: Walker Information, 2002.

Employees expect business to actively help build a better society and, like consumers, employees reward those that do (see Exhibit 2.2).

The Council on Foundations cited two additional overall benefits of good corporate citizenship, the benefits of improved employee morale and improved customer relationships already mentioned. They found that such programs, particularly when visible and rational:

- Improve business performance, citing improved bottom-line returns, increases in competitive advantage, and better cross-functional integration.

- Enhance marketing efforts by helping to create a positive image, support higher prestige prices, and boost government affairs activities.

## THE VALUE OF QUALITY

During the 1980s and 1990s, *quality* was *the* catchword for progressive businesses in every sector. Not only was it a catchword, but it was taken seriously, studied, and assimilated into most business plans. Times have changed, it's clear, especially when it comes to businesses committing to quality in their corporate citizenship.

There was a time when quality went beyond a company's efforts to become ISO certified. The standard for quality was derived more universally from the Baldrige National

Quality Program. Baldrige calls for two key points of quality to be addressed and met before any others: "Organizational Leadership" and "Public Responsibility and Citizenship." Organizational leadership requires an uncompromising commitment of management to reaching quality goals throughout the company. The public responsibility and citizenship category covers areas that range from safety to ethics.

Another part—the essence of operations for nonprofits, but not necessarily for industry and commerce—is support of key communities. The criteria for excellence specifically state that "[t]his typically includes efforts by the organization to support and strengthen key communities of strategic importance to the organizations such as community services, education, health care, the environment . . . ." If quality is not achieved in these areas, it cannot be achieved in other parts of the operation.

The first step is leadership: making the commitment to quality from the top, then instilling that commitment throughout the company, and then taking it beyond the company to the community. Leaders like you must take that step to achieve comprehensive quality in your company. You're moving in that direction with this book.

## When to Start a Program

### From the Start

The best time to start a corporate citizenship program is when you're writing your business plan. That way, you can incorporate corporate citizenship into every part of your operations. Even at the very early stages of building your business, even if you think you can't afford it, there are ways of using this tool to cultivate customers.

Let's take the example of the two-person website-design shop. A husband and wife are working out of the basement of their home. They get a contract to design a website for a home-alarm manufacturer and installer. The contract is valued at $5,000. During the course of doing business, the website designers learn that the client sits on the board of the local chapter of the Cerebral Palsy Society, because his grandson suffers from that condition.

The client has been pleased by the product and refers a supplier to the designers. Most businesses would give the alarm company a referral fee. All the designers can afford is $100, which isn't really a significant amount to a company with many millions in revenues each year. Sending flowers or a plant is another option, but sending a $100 donation to the Cerebral Palsy Society is certain to make a bigger impression on the client, and may even give the designer an entrée to the charity as a future client. Charities want to do business with their donors.

The website design company is small and doesn't need a sophisticated plan for charitable contributions. Its policy is simply to give 2 percent of each contract to a charity that appeals to the client in the client's name, or to make a donation in lieu of a referral fee or gift.

## When Requests Require Time

Most business owners find that the majority of their requests come from three sources: employees, customers, and the community at large.

If you have no employees, that is not an issue.

If you have only a small number of employees (say, less than 100), that probably is not a major issue either. Most employees in smaller operations will ask the boss for the favor of a donation only once a year or less. In such cases, the owner can generally address the request quickly, if not on the spot.

Similarly, when there is only a small client base, the requests are not frequent and the business owner is anxious to say yes to cultivate a good relationship.

When your employees number in the hundreds and so do your customers, if each one asks but once a year, it still adds up to dozens of requests a week. It's virtually impossible for one or two people to give measured consideration to each request. Some system must be put in place to screen and evaluate requests, and procedures instituted to minimize any negative repercussions of rejections.

## When Donation Dollars Grow

When your company was new and its donations were in the hundreds of dollars, they were easy to track; they could simply be lumped under *miscellaneous* or even *petty cash*. When donation dollars grow into the five and even six figures (or beyond), they have a real impact on your bottom line and should receive the same kind of consideration and planning as do other budget items of the same size.

I've always found it amazing that banks will make new business owners bare their financial souls in order to get even a small loan. Yet, they often make four-figure charitable donations without asking even the simplest questions about the organization's financial operations, finding out its administrative practices, or checking out who is involved in its governance. A donation is an investment—a social investment. Your business should take the same care in making these kinds of investments as you do in buying new office equipment or any capital expenditure of equivalent value.

## During Mergers and Acquisitions

Mergers and acquisitions are times to do things differently and to create new corporate cultures. Acquired companies may have policies and procedures for corporate citizenship that differ sharply from those of the purchasing company. Although issues of corporate citizenship never make or break a deal for merger or acquisition, they can make a difference in the eventual success of the new company.

This was true in the case of Norwest Bank's acquisition of Wells Fargo. Norwest had a highly decentralized system whereby charitable donations were decided upon at the branch-bank level. Wells Fargo made all decisions at its headquarters. It took more than a year for the new Wells Fargo Foundation and banks to realign the old Wells Fargo banks and train managers into the Norwest Banks model of independent granting.

Mergers and acquisitions are nightmares for most charities. They fear that they will lose contributions from a donor company if it is acquired. They fear that the sum of the donation from two merged companies will not equal the separate donations from the prior independent donors. Sometimes these worst-case scenarios become real. At other times, according to the "Mergers: Implications for Corporate Philanthropy and the Community" report, an acquisition may actually improve a company's giving when the company receives an influx of capital and profits improve.[7]

## At Changes in Leadership

A change in leadership may be a generational one for a family business, a promotion from inside, or a recruitment of a new CEO for a public company. Whatever form the change takes, such events are good times to take a new look at how corporate citizenship is conducted and start a program or revitalize an old one.

The charitable organizations that the leader favors for the program can set the tone for the entire organization, from the executive suite to the production floor to the sales environment. Your leadership and participation on nonprofit boards can bring new business to the company and new opportunities for involvement by your employees at all levels. If you recognize one or more of these situations in your company, it's time for you to start putting together a strategic plan for corporate citizenship.

## CHAPTER 3

# Who Gives?

In 2002, a coalition of 14 Minnesota businesses and associations, called the Building Business Investment in Community (BBIC), issued a report on the state of business giving and volunteerism.[1] Minnesota has historically been toward the top regarding business and personal philanthropy, so it is worthwhile for businesses across the nation to look at these results, both as benchmarks to aim at, and for some important lessons to be learned from reading between the report's lines. The BBIC report divided companies into four groups:

1. Very small, with fewer than 20 employees, including one-person shops and family farms
2. Small businesses, 20–99 employees
3. Medium businesses, 100–499 employees
4. Large businesses, 500+ employees

BBIC's key findings showed that giving and community involvement were widespread and varied. Most businesses give cash, with 88 percent of companies with more than 20 employees donating; very small business was not far behind, with 72 percent giving cash. Another key point in the BBIC study was that the focus of giving was local, stressing the importance of community ties. Giving back to the community was the main motivating factor, as business owners recognized that giving also benefits business.

Are any business donors more likely to give, or is any particular group more generous than another?

## WOMEN IN BUSINESS

The National Foundation for Women Business Owners[2] reports that in 1999, the United States had about 9.1 million woman-owned firms, employing almost 28 million people and generating more than \$3.2 trillion in revenue. The percentage of their net worth given to charity beats out corporations, corporate and private foundations, and men-owned businesses.

The *Chronicle of Philanthropy* reported that, on a proportional basis, women who own businesses are the most generous donors to nonprofit organizations.[3] Most women who read the report probably yawned and waved it off with a remark like "But of *course!*" The way they gave was not always recognized as valuable by the powerful establishment, unfortunately. Women volunteered. When women had little earning power, volunteering was a way of giving back.

BBIC found that 70 percent of businesses with 20 or more employees reported that they offer or encourage employees to volunteer. Those volunteer hours can add up to a bundle of cash saved, as any nonprofit executive director can tell you. The range of value for each volunteer hour is now pegged at between \$13 and \$15.50.

The dollar value of women's volunteer time is even more accentuated when compared with the volunteer time of men. Independent Sector, the economic research institute (*www.indepsec.org*), reported in 1999 that 62 percent of women give time, as contrasted with 49 percent of men.[4] This shows a further widening of the philanthropic gender gap.

When it comes to cash and other financial assets, the *Chronicle* study concluded, women are donating at about the same rate—2.1 percent—as men. These percentages can be deceiving. Even before the great spurt in market value (which has not been totally lost), the average net worth of a wealthy woman was slightly higher than that of a wealthy man. Hence, that 2.1 percent results in more money for philanthropy from women. Combining the cash and the value of volunteer hours, successful businesswomen are leaving their male counterparts eating their dust (gold dust, that is!).

Women have always been valued as fundraisers. Too often, however, they were invited to join committees because as wives they were a conduit to their husbands' wealth and influence. Now, savvy businesswomen are recruited to governing boards on the basis of their own assets, financial and personal.

Now we know that women in business give more financially for philanthropy. The value of their volunteer time adds to the equation. Does it then follow that the kinds of things they support differ from their male peers? If they give more, do they also give in different ways?

Successful businesswomen have similar philanthropic priorities, according to Judy Bloom, president of Resourceful Women (*www.rw.org*). They typically give about three-quarters of their philanthropic budget to causes addressing women and girls. This bodes well for these organizations in our communities. As time goes by and more women gain success in business, such groups can expect to see their support and programming increase and improve.

We can conclude from this last fact that women tend to *plan* their giving. The Women's Philanthropy Institute (www.women-philanthropy.org) observes that women:

- Prefer new projects to existing causes.
- Fund specific projects instead of unrestricted programming.

- Gravitate toward scholarships and social programs.
- Prefer to be part of a larger campaign rather than making isolated gifts.
- Want continual updates on how money is being spent.
- Are not as comfortable as men with multiyear pledges.
- Are not as responsive as men in matching what others have contributed.

Giving circles—based on the model of investment clubs—are a new feminist path for philanthropy. The investments are social and the payoffs are improvements in people's lives and the overall quality of life for a community. Giving circles seem to be growing in geographic concentric circles, emanating from centers such as Detroit.

The woman who is successful in business gives more, gives differently, and plans her giving. The tables are turned on men when it comes to philanthropy.

## Big Business

Big business, "Corporate America," learned long ago that big giving was good for business. The genesis and philosophies of the foundations supported by US Steel, Chase Manhattan, and the like didn't come about by committee; it was their far-sighted multi-millionaire founders who set the agenda and the tone for these institutions and made examples for generations of others to follow.

Andrew Carnegie put his name on hundreds of libraries across the entire nation at the turn of the 20th century. Today, most cities with major hospitals serving large numbers of seriously ill pediatric patients host a Ronald McDonald House to shelter children who are undergoing long-term treatment, along with their concerned parents. The Ford Motor Company has a foundation dedicated to providing college scholarships for the children of the company's employees.

Big business sets the standard for all business when it comes to philanthropy. The creators of the Minnesota Principles and the leadership of the Caux Round Table have all been representatives of U.S. *Forbes 500* companies and their international counterparts.

Consequently, the impact of unethical or illegal business behavior goes far beyond the company's bottom line. The whole economy is affected when there is a downturn, as the recession at the beginning of this century proves. That the economic downturn is hurting people at the lowest end of our local economy is no surprise. But exactly how it's hurting them in the post-welfare reform world often is not understood.

Most of us know that when low-wage workers lose jobs or hours, it can make the difference between paying rent and buying food, or not. How they cope with that dilemma is different today than it was in the late 1990s when the stock market was soaring. The poor and working poor could, until recently, count on services provided by a variety of nonprofit organizations to provide a few days' worth of food, a week of shelter, or job training.

Nonprofits have been hit doubly hard in these times, as newspapers and magazines across the nation report. Not only are donations down, but their endowments and reserves have shrunk along with individual investments. Donor organizations, such as foundations, also have seen their endowments shrink. The *Chronicle of Philanthropy* estimated that in 2002 the top 10 national foundations lost anywhere from 1.5 to 30 percent of the value of their endowments.[5]

Fewer resources to nonprofits can mean fewer staff and other services. It's easy to see what that means for clients of social service organizations. But what does it mean for the larger community, and the business community in particular? What's the business connection?

Let's look at a typical small nonprofit in a Minneapolis suburb, Bridging, that serves as a free furniture and home products bank. Its clients include women who have been forced to leave their homes due to abuse, and persons who have been living in shelters for the homeless. Bridging has eight full-time employees and a payroll of $330,000, including benefits. It's a tight budget by anyone's standards. Nevertheless, Bridging's payroll still translates into a lot of commerce for local merchants and service companies from Bridging's employees.

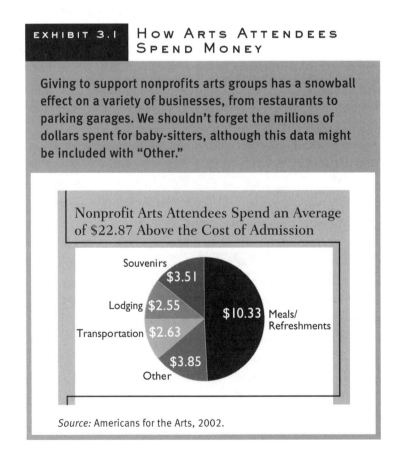

**EXHIBIT 3.1    HOW ARTS ATTENDEES SPEND MONEY**

Giving to support nonprofits arts groups has a snowball effect on a variety of businesses, from restaurants to parking garages. We shouldn't forget the millions of dollars spent for baby-sitters, although this data might be included with "Other."

Nonprofit Arts Attendees Spend an Average of $22.87 Above the Cost of Admission

Souvenirs $3.51
Lodging $2.55
Transportation $2.63
Other $3.85
Meals/Refreshments $10.33

*Source:* Americans for the Arts, 2002.

Multiply Bridging by the thousands of food pantries, battered women's shelters, and other agencies serving the poor in our country, and the economic impact is clear. If each of these organizations loses only one or two employees, the ripple effect can be considerable.

Here's another slant on the implications of the economic slowdown for another non-profit sector: the arts. In its 2002 report on the economic impact of nonprofit arts organizations and their audiences, Americans for the Arts reports that attendance at arts events generates related commerce for other businesses (such as hotels, restaurants, and parking garages) to the tune of $22.87 per person per event—not including the cost of admission. Out-of-towners spend even more (see Exhibit 3.1).[6]

When business does not respond adequately to nonprofits during times of crisis, it may find that the local services their employees and customers have counted on in the past will not be there to serve them when the downturn is over.

## Small and Mid-Market Businesses

The BBIC report showed that medium-sized businesses participate in giving at nearly the same rate that big business does. But it also showed that only 43 percent of them have formal budgets or plans for corporate citizenship donations and activities. This contrasts with 67 percent of large companies.[7] The lesson? If you want to grow and be a big business, then you should get this part of your business into your *business plan*.

Why don't many businesses include corporate citizenship in their business plans? First of all, most entrepreneurs start businesses to make money. Many entrepreneurs may think about giving on a personal level, out of the profits they receive from a successful business. Giving money away is just not part of their business plans. Secondly, making giving a part of doing business is not something that appears prominently in the curriculum of most business schools. It's not taught. Thirdly, smaller businesses may think, as to giving, that there's nothing in it for them. This is where they are wrong. They can truly benefit from learning how to give well and wisely. Then they can take what they've learned, incorporate it into their business plans, and do well by doing good.

What can any business, large or small, accomplish by making a plan for giving? On the most fundamental level, giving to qualified nonprofit organizations will generate tax deductions. All businesses give to charities on an involuntary basis, whether they know it or not. Some of their tax dollars are granted by government agencies to a variety of nonprofit groups. A business owner may or may not agree with which group is getting how much. Voluntary donations are tax-deductible and give you the choice as to how your donation is used.

Looking internally, a rational giving plan can make a real difference in employee morale. When the boss makes all the decisions without a formal policy, giving can be seen as arbitrary, and it may well be so. Well-defined policies and procedures eliminate vagaries and the appearance of favoritism when employees ask management to support their personal causes. Businesses uneducated in giving may also use personnel inefficiently to administer the grants they do make. That may cost them more than the value of the grants they make to charities.

Smart giving can transform business philanthropy into social investing. Wise, planned social investments will reflect the company's values and goals, help to create a community that offers a better quality of life for employees, and build an economy that provides a stronger market for the company's products and services. Just as individuals and businesses develop financial investment plans to ensure their own stability and growth, businesses need to learn what is best for them and their communities as they create social investment plans. Is the company strictly local in its production and sales? Are there particular institutions that provide entry-level employees? A business can make social investments that make sense in these areas.

A basic tenet of ethical business is delivering value for the purchase price. Purchasing managers do comparison shopping to make sure that the company is getting the most for its investment. Why should it be any different when a company is making a social investment? Which organization is doing the best job in its field? On the one hand, putting money into a sure thing avoids the risk of the organization losing or abusing the investment. On the other hand, a wise social investment could help make or break a new initiative.

How can a business make sure it gets what it deserves for its investment? First, it can learn about giving. For example, the Association of Fundraising Professionals has issued a Donor's Bill of Rights (discussed in Part Two of this book).

How about publicity and recognition for giving? If a company wants visibility, that should be part of its giving strategy. Charities themselves and many business associations grant awards to good citizen members. A company that doesn't give doesn't win such awards.

The new wealth in much of today's economy rests with owners of growing New Economy businesses. Look at the donor list in the program of your local orchestra or art museum and you'll see that the names of many of the fast-growth companies are missing. These business owners must learn how to give and give wisely. They must learn which organizations exist that promote the company's mission. They can observe the example of others that have successful partnerships with nonprofit groups. All this will lead to making a plan to give and sticking to it.

How do you make that plan? Read on.

# PART TWO

# Practical Guidance for Planning Your Program

## CHAPTER 4

# Choosing the Decision Makers and Procedures

**M**ost companies don't create a corporate citizenship plan because they have no experience in doing it and don't know what their options are. Often, activities happen on an *ad hoc* basis and decisions are arbitrary.

Corporate citizenship activities are viewed as a necessary burden, and the responsibility for carrying them out is often delegated to people well outside the executive suite. In this case, two things can happen: Either (1) the employee in charge enjoys the activities and responsibilities, or (2) the employee resents having the job foisted upon her. She's busy with other charges and tasks and isn't given the authority or the means to do a good job, and she has nothing to say about what kinds of decisions are made, how they are made, or where the money will go. And, although it's seldom in her job description, performance in this area is included in her evaluation. In too many companies, it's the latter scenario that's played out.

Choosing the right people—a "steering committee"—to put the plan together is the first step in avoiding this situation, and is key to the long-term success of the program. Choosing the steering committee members for your corporate citizenship program is an activity that takes place twice in the planning process: first, when you are drawing the outlines of policies and procedures; and second, when the plan is implemented.

Some of the decision-making issues vary according to the kind of business structure you are dealing with. Those are addressed separately later in this chapter. The common issues are addressed under one heading.

## IDENTIFYING THE POLICY MAKERS

When you are deciding on the decision makers, look at the business and legal structure of the company and the current company culture. Is yours a closely held business, an employee-owned company (EOC), or a public company?

## Questions for Closely Held Businesses '

**Family-Owned Businesses**    Choosing decision makers is important not only for the company, but also for the sake of the family of which the company is an extension. It can make the family a functional, cohesive unit for generations, or break it and the business.

Does the family want to be the sole arbiter of what the company's citizenship policies should be? If so, which family members should be involved in the formulation of the plan?

### *Questions*

1. Should only members of the family who are actively employed by the company be involved in setting up the plan? How about retirees?

2. Should only members of the family who currently serve on the board or are members of management be involved? (In a larger company that is several generations old, this might keep the size of the committee manageable.)

3. What about spouses? No one wants to think about divorce, but it can happen, and its effect on the company's giving policy must be considered, especially if the estranged spouse has been active in the company's giving program.

4. If both spouses are employees or otherwise qualified shareholders, should *both* of them be allowed to be engaged in the decision-making process, while other family-owner couples only have one representative? (This situation can be compared to how Congress is set up, with all states having equal representation in the Senate, but the more populous states having greater representation in the House.)

5. Can you give weight or partial votes to family members who are not actively engaged in the business but are shareholders? If they are living in communities where company operations are present, they may look to the company giving program as a substitute for their own philanthropy.

6. Do you want to put restrictions on participation by shareholders who are not company employees (for example, age or educational standards)? The 16-year-old who is working for the company after school or during the summer will have a bigger stake in the company than her 16-year-old cousin who lives out of town. You may not want the 30-year-old who never finished college and is living off his income from the company to be involved in the company's citizenship program (if he even has any desire to do so).

7. Does the family want non-family members involved in the discussion (for example, top non-family managers)? Should they be given equal decision-making consideration? Those who have been with the company for a long time may have special insights into what makes sense regarding contributions.

8. Should you bring in members of the younger generation, at least for discussions? If you do, they can then observe and learn the serious and thoughtful way in which

giving decisions are made, and be better prepared to take their place when their turn arrives.

**EOCs**  Employee-owned companies might find it easier to follow the pattern of their management model when starting to develop a corporate citizenship plan. The established business plan already demonstrates how much authority each employee-owner exerts in the company's structure. Even so, here are some seminal questions:

### Questions

1.  If there are non-owner employees, should they be allowed to participate in the policy-setting meeting(s)? Certainly, they should understand that it is only the generosity of owners that permits them to participate in policy making at any level, because they are not owners. This decision may be easier if it is a small company and the numbers of owners and non-owners are similar, or if owners far outnumber non-owners. A representative or two from the non-owner camp would not tip the scales significantly if it came to a showdown between the two interests. When non-owners far outnumber owners, however, they should not be overrepresented in policy making without significant consideration of the ramifications, just as in public companies.

2.  Should decision-maker slots be restricted to those holding a minimum number of shares? This depends on the total number of shares. When there are few shares, it is easy to let everyone participate. When thousands of shares are outstanding, numbers and percentages can become significant in terms of influence and weight of votes.

3.  If there is no minimum number of shares, what should be the standard? Seniority? Consider the janitor who has been with the company for 28 years and the head of sales who has been a co-owner for 10. What is their relative value to the company? What perspectives do they have on company operations, both internal and external? Should title/management level be your standard? (If your company is instituting the program largely for reasons of internal morale, it would be a bad decision to go this route.)

## Questions for Public Companies

Publicly held companies have special corporate citizenship responsibilities, and therefore must plan their citizenship program with particular care. The onus for good policy falls particularly heavily on the initial decision makers.

One of the key responsibilities of corporate management is to provide a return on investment for shareholders. For that reason, many companies choose *not* to make any donations to charity from the company checkbook. Rather, they distribute higher dividends to shareholders and allow *them* to make donations to the charities of their choice.

Others distance themselves from the decision-making process by forfeiting their responsibilities to an independent or semi-independent company foundation. The General Mills Foundation is a prime example. Each year, the company donates a portion of its profits or stock to its foundation to create or add to an endowment, from which 5 percent is donated annually to charity. Even with an independent foundation, though, several representatives from the company usually sit on the board of trustees. Setting up a company foundation is an expensive process, both legally and administratively. Few middle-market companies can do so, although some still choose that route.

Most medium-sized companies, like those surveyed in the BBIC project, end up giving out of their annual profits. After looking at some of the questions in the preceding lists, they can also start out asking questions like these:

### Questions

1.   Who in management should be involved in setting the policy and procedure plan?
2.   Should board members who are not employees be invited to participate?
3.   Do you want to weight the voting according to position in management?
4.   Do you want to have equal representation among different levels of labor and management, or will you have proportional representation?

   •   How will representation be allocated between exempt and nonexempt employees?
   •   How will the company's various divisions/departments be represented?
   •   Shall the participants be selected or nominated by management?
   •   Shall the participants be selected by seniority or other criteria?

## General Questions and Considerations

Once the criteria for the membership of the policy-making committee have been decided and the actual committee members have been selected (between three and ten members is a good, workable size), the process of creating policies and procedures can commence. The process should take between three and six hours, in one or two meetings. The questions and issues for consideration are discussed in following chapters.

But we are not done with choosing decision makers yet. Once the policies and procedures are set, the steering committee can choose to continue as an operating committee, or it can set the criteria and directions for a new operating committee to conduct the program on an ongoing basis. In the latter case, the members should revisit the questions asked when the steering committee was being formed, and then consider some additional questions.

   •   Shall you have terms of service on the committee? How long should a term be? Annual, biannual, permanent? If people have permanent positions, they can gain undue influence; if they are rotated out annually, the committee will suffer a lack of experience and institutional memory.

- Do you want anyone from outside the company to sit on the committee, or should there be some special considerations for committee composition? Aside from those mentioned earlier, consider others who might bring particular insights to decision making:
    - Should you try to ensure that there is gender or age balance among committee members?
    - If you have employees spread across different locations, how much geographic representation do you want?
    - If you sponsor scholarships or awards, would it be helpful to have past winners participate in selecting the next ones?
    - Would asking a community representative to assist you in your decisions be a good idea if you are trying to open a new market in that area?
    - Would you be willing to have company interns sit in on your meetings? If the supervisor of the job the intern is learning might qualify for a seat on the committee, wouldn't this be a way of teaching the intern about the responsibilities and processes of good corporate citizenship?

With your steering committee in place, you can integrate your decisions about operating-committee policy into the comprehensive plan you are about to complete.

## Conducting the Grants Meeting

Well in advance of the first grants meeting, each member of the committee should receive a copy of all the policies and procedures, including sample copies of application forms, evaluation forms, and the like. This is especially important for members who were not part of the steering committee that created the documents. They should be informed as to whom to contact if they have questions about any part of the procedure. As old members cycle off the committee and new ones are added, each new member should be paired with a continuing member, to help get the new members up to speed on committee operations.

Committee members should receive copies of all requests and related materials, and should be given ample time to review them before the meeting when they will be under consideration for funding (see Chapter 6 on scheduling). Making decisions without thoughtful review puts your company in a worse position than before you established the committee. Instead of one person making arbitrary decisions, there will be a committee of several persons making arbitrary decisions.

A thorough examination of requests should stimulate discussion on the assets and liabilities of each proposal. Even if your budget exceeds the amount of dollars requested at any given meeting, there should be no automatic, rubber-stamped approvals of grants.

Similarly, informed discussion will help avoid the situation in which one member of the committee dominates the decision-making process. When selecting committee members, attention should be paid to avoiding any undue influence or conflict of interest between decision makers and those who are seeking funding.

Taking minutes is also essential. Documenting the discussion and maintaining records of requests and grants communications is important should legal questions arise in the future regarding the donations. This might sound extreme, but there are too many cases of questionable charitable intent on record, which might negate the tax deductibility of a donation, to take this step lightly. For example, in the late 1980s, the University of Minnesota Foundation undertook a major capital campaign to endow professorial positions. Reporters on the local newspaper got some information that led them to believe that corporate donors had been granted exceptional powers to choose the recipients of these endowed chairs. After months of investigation and examination of tens of thousands of pages of documents (with the concomitant expenditure of time, effort, and money), the allegations were found to be entirely baseless.

## Checklist of Options/Considerations

Many of the choices suggested for public companies should be considered by EOCs and family-owned companies as well.

### *Public Companies*

*Representation*

- ❐ Exempt only?
- ❐ Nonexempt/union?
- ❐ From various departments/divisions?
- ❐ Gender balance?
- ❐ From different geographic areas?
- ❐ From different parts of your stakeholder community:
    - ❐ Owners/stockholders?
    - ❐ Community representatives?
    - ❐ Board members?
    - ❐ Customers?

*Selection/Nomination Process*

- ❐ By seniority
- ❐ By senior management
- ❐ By existing committee members
- ❐ By self-selected volunteers

*Vote Weighting*

- ❐  Management position
- ❐  Equal weight/democratic

*Terms*

- ❐  Annual
- ❐  Biannual
- ❐  Permanent
- ❐  Staggered terms to maintain continuity

### *Family/Closely Held Companies*

- ❐  Actively employed family members
- ❐  Retirees
- ❐  Family members not engaged in the business
- ❐  Spouses
- ❐  Age/educational limitations
- ❐  Non-family managers

### *Employee-Owned Companies (EOCs)*

- ❐  Participation by nonowner employees
- ❐  Minimum shares for participation in policy making
- ❐  Selection by seniority
- ❐  Selection by title

## CHAPTER 5

# Defining the Mission

Most businesses have a mission statement. The mission statement lays out what the company intends to do and how it intends to do it. Whether stated or unstated, one part of the mission of the company is *always to make money.*

One of my favorite true stories is that of a speech given by Lifecore Biomedical's president and CEO, Dr. James Brakke. Dr. Brakke had been invited by the University of Minnesota BioProcess Technology Institute to address a group of more than 100 undergraduate biology students at the university for a special conference. This was during a time of renewed student social activism and social awareness.

"Why did I decide to go into business instead of university research?" was Dr. Brakke's rhetorical question to the students. "Why? So I could make lots of *money!*" There was an audible gasp from the audience after Brakke's venomous stress on that last word. He waited for the pregnant pause to pass. "Why do I want to make all that money?" he continued. "So that I could give it all away!"

Lifecore Biomedical, a manufacturer of medical and surgical materials, has set up a company foundation. The mission of the company is to *make* money, and the mission of the foundation is to *give* money away.

As we said before, your company does not have to create a separate foundation to be able to give money away. But your corporate citizenship program should have its own separate, but related, mission statement for giving.

Why do I insist that the "giving" mission be related to the "making" mission? The Council on Foundations has discovered that such programs, particularly when *visible* and *rational:*

- Improve business performance. The Council cited improved bottom-line returns, increases in competitive advantage, and better cross-functional integration.

- Enhance marketing efforts by helping to create a positive image.

- Support higher prestige prices.
- Boost government affairs activities.[1]

All this boils down to making a connection between the company's products, services, and market for making money and the charitable causes it will support.

Lucky is the Lifecore Biomedical company, whose products address specific health conditions. This firm can easily identify health-related organizations or educational institutions that share concerns about advancing research into treatment, prevention, and cure of diseases that their company's products affect.

This is not always easy when you're a general widget maker. Your company has a couple hundred production employees, virtually all in the same location, and a highly-scattered sales force that sells widgets to a vast number of industries. Your challenge, then, must be to focus your mission on your most important constituency. It is up to you to decide who that constituency is: your employees, your shareholders, your customers, your community, and so on. Then you must focus your mission around that constituency and their concerns.

## CREATING A CORPORATE CITIZENSHIP MISSION STATEMENT

Here are a few examples of corporate citizenship program mission statements. Some other good examples can be found in Appendix A.

### ABC Company (Privately Held Publisher and Printer)

*The ABC Company's Community Relations Program will create a collaborative, inclusive environment for our employee community, fostering pride in our companies and respect for co-workers to inspire them to ever-higher levels of personal and professional excellence. ABC Company wants to be recognized for our excellence and respected for our quality as the supplier, employer, and neighbor of choice. Our Community Relations Program will consistently support and enhance the Mission Statement of the ABC Company to accelerate literacy, expand educational opportunities, and improve and protect the global environment.*

### DEF Corporation (Small Public High-Technology Manufacturer)

*DEF Corporation's Corporate Citizenship Program is an effort in which the company and its employees together make a difference in peoples' lives through voluntary service and financial support. The following policies and procedures are meant as guidelines for DEF Corporation employees. In keeping with DEF's core values, the company wishes to respect the employees' own wisdom and autonomy in guiding this program to reflect the unique abilities of each employee and the equally unique culture and needs of every community where DEF has a presence.*

### GHI Bank (Privately Held Bank)

*GHI Bank's Community Involvement Program is committed to fostering a bank team who is proud and pleased to work for GHI Bank. The bank also strives to be a visible and contributing member of the community. GHI Bank's Community Involvement Program's goal is to help make the communities in which we do business stronger by supporting the charitable organizations and those in need in our market areas. Programs supported by GHI Bank's Community Involvement Program should strive to develop integrity, account-ability, responsibility, and community growth or strengthen families.*

Each of these statements shares several characteristics:

- They are short. Your mission statement should be no longer than five sentences. If you have more text, then consider adding a preamble to your charitable giving plan document. That preamble may contain information on the company's history or a statement about the values of the company's founder as a tribute.

- They identify target constituencies: community, employees, and the like. This makes it clear what your priorities are, helps you decide on whom you will support by your giving, and clarifies who will be involved in your decision-making process.

- They state the core values that the program wants to embody and to promote. This is the basis of the screening program of your corporate citizenship program, and can stimulate the most soul-searching for your committee. Trying to discern whether a program characterizes your values, on the basis of a short written application form, can be challenging. For this reason, the more involvement the members of your committee have with the community and the organizations you eventually end up supporting, the easier it will be for you to see the consistencies in values between the charities and your company.

It's my experience that creating the mission statement is always the most difficult part of the planning process. It will likely take an initial 45 minutes or so. Keep the mission literally in clear sight (use a whiteboard or sheets of newsprint) while conducting the rest of your planning meeting, so that you can:

- Refer to it and keep the rest of your plan consistent with it. If you don't, you will end up in the same situation you started with: making arbitrary decisions about thousands of dollars.

- Tweak it as the rest of your plan unfolds. There is nothing wrong with changing your mission statement as the discussion develops. New ideas, attitudes, and objectives are bound to arise during the planning process. The mission statement is not immutable over time, either. As your company grows and changes, so might your mission change.

The best examples of this sort of mission change are two well-known nonprofits: the March of Dimes and CARE. The March of Dimes was started after World War II to win a different war, the one against polio. With the development of the Salk vaccine, the mission was accomplished. The March of Dimes could have marched off into the sunset, feeling proud of its work. Instead, the trustees looked at the research infrastructure and fundraising capacity they had built and chose to redirect the organization's mission to a new challenge: birth defects.

Similarly, CARE was started after World War II to provide relief packages to European war victims. During the process, it became involved in reconstruction. By the time the late 1960s rolled around, European reconstruction had been completed, so CARE focused its expertise on the developing Third World. Its mission was no less humanitarian, but it was aimed at different targets.

A prime example of a radical change in business plans for a profit-making institution is the Westinghouse Corporation. Readers over the age of 40 will associate Westinghouse with electricity and electrical devices such as frying pans, fans, and other household items. When the company could not compete with foreign producers, it reinvented itself. The company is thriving, but has changed its focus completely from being a consumer products manufacturer to being a service and research provider to large public and private utilities.

## Starting the Discussion on Mission

Here are some initial questions you might ask to begin the mission discussion:

- *Do we want our company's philanthropic mission to be tied to our products/services?* If your products or services are esoteric or have a highly limited market, it may be a good idea to concentrate on a different segment of your business's shareholders: your local community or something tied to your company's name. If your company's name is Falcon Diversified Products, your mission might focus on environmental protection, particularly endangered avian species.

- *Do we want our philanthropic mission to go beyond the interests of the owners?* This tests the generosity of owners of closely held companies. How much of this money (that truly is their own) are they willing to entrust to others who might use it for purposes that are diametrically opposed to the owners' personal interests and values? The discussion might lead to the development of a separate corporate foundation that uses a major donation from the owner as an initial endowment, but is regularly supplemented by donations from employees.

- *Do we want our philanthropic mission to go beyond the interests of the employees?* Your employees may have limited interests when it comes to company giving, particularly if yours is a smaller business. Depending on your goals for the program, the board of directors can take the lead and set the direction, following the other steps in this book.

- *What do we want to accomplish* internally *that relates to our giving to groups* external *to the company?* Here is where the terms *mission* and *vision* often can be blurred or interchanged. You may want to call an internal mission statement (about what you want to accomplish within your company) your *vision statement* and another (what you want to accomplish for society) your *mission statement.* What you call them is up to you, but your program's purpose should be both introspective and universal.

Each member of the team that is involved in creating these statements will be bringing his or her own personal experiences and values to the table. It is important to recognize, acknowledge, and respect these. However, it is equally important to emphasize that they may not be identical to or even consistent with the company's values and priorities.

A good exercise that illustrates this point is to go around the table and ask each person to name the last charity or cause to which they wrote a check that was not their house of worship or their alma mater. Then ask them if they felt that this would be an appropriate cause for the company to support. In the majority of cases, even though the causes are worthy for those individuals or society, they would not be logical candidates for company support. For example, a food processor with a regional market in the South would be hard put to justify support of a project to save an endangered species in the Pacific Northwest.

## CHECKLIST

What are the key values that drive your company, or that you would like to see drive this program? Use this list as a catalyst for your committee to brainstorm others that relate to your company's unique situation. Ask each committee member to name five words he or she feels represent the company's current values or values the member would like to see the company embrace. Keep a tally of how many times each word appears on the list, and then create your mission/vision statement from the top three to five values.

- ❏ Quality
- ❏ Respect
- ❏ Service
- ❏ Responsibility
- ❏ Creativity
- ❏ Diversity
- ❏ Communication
- ❏ Honesty
- ❏ Fairness
- ❏ Community
- ❏ Professionalism

- ☐ Trust
- ☐ Caring
- ☐ Citizenship
- ☐ Intelligence
- ☐ Education
- ☐ Skill
- ☐ Liberalism
- ☐ Conservatism
- ☐ Purity
- ☐ Integrity
- ☐ Accountability
- ☐ Excellence
- ☐ Loyalty

## CHAPTER 6

# Scheduling

In every aspect of American life today, and certainly in business, the most valuable commodity is time. One of the reasons to develop a plan for your corporate citizenship program is to save time. Without a plan, how are you wasting your time?

Picture yourself in this scenario: You are the CEO of your company, and you are paid, on a salary basis alone, $300,000 per year. That translates to about $6,000 per week, or $150 per hour for your 40-hour workweek (of course, we know that you work *far* more than *that!*).

Each week, you get about six requests for contributions of one kind or another. A client asks you to buy a hole at the charity golf tournament his company is sponsoring. A valued production employee asks the company to underwrite the cost of the high school band's travel to perform in a prestigious parade. The chair of the Chamber of Commerce scholarship committee asks for an increase in your pledge over last year. If you give only 10 minutes of consideration time to each request each week, you have already "given away" $150 to charity that is doing nobody any good, and indeed is losing money for your company because your time has been diverted from helping to create profits. Multiply that $150 by 52 weeks, and you have wasted $7,800 worth of your time and your company's potential profits. Multiply that again by the number and salaries of others who serve on the corporate citizenship committee, and you'll see it adds up to a substantial bite out of profits.

There are two objectives in scheduling corporate citizenship meetings:

1. To minimize the time spent in this arena for those with decision-making powers.
2. To maximize the effectiveness of the decisions made.

## SCHEDULING OPTIONS

There are three basic ways to schedule the committee's meetings, and each has its positives and negatives. How you choose to set the meetings will depend largely on the mission of your program.

## Annual Meeting

*Pros*    Scheduling your giving to be done once a year is the easiest way. It also is probably the most time-efficient as well.

Your company, be it public or private, has an annual shareholders meeting. You have many reports to prepare and present. You know that all of your most concerned and involved stakeholders will be there or will be looking forward to receiving the written report. If you tack on a discussion of corporate citizenship to other meetings, or schedule it as another of the essential discussions in preparation for the annual meeting, you will minimize time spent in various ways: If members are coming to the meeting from various locations, they will spend less travel time. If you set limits to the number of requests for consideration at the meeting, this can further minimize preparation and deliberation time.

*Cons*    First, community needs and charitable causes seldom turn on fixed calendar dates. If your annual meeting is held in June, and then a community disaster occurs in August, will you really want to wait until the next June to decide whether to contribute to a recovery fund? Clearly not, as the effectiveness of your donation is tied to the urgency of the event.

Second, given a similar timing scenario, if your company is requested in August to sponsor an event in April that has clear opportunities for visibility, recognition, and even sales potential, you will lose the chance to take advantage of the situation by waiting until the annual meeting.

**Alternative Options**    Many companies make allowances for such situations by adopting alternative policies.

**Executive Prerogative**    When emergency situations arise, the executive is allowed to make limited donations without consulting the committee. A portion of the program budget is set aside for these requests. With another strategy, contributions made by the executive for emergencies can be taken from other sources of profit or revenue, so as to safeguard funds earmarked for targeted philanthropy.

Contributions to emergency funds must be examined carefully for their tax-exempt qualifications. Many emergency funds set up to assist individuals in dire medical or personal straits do not have tax-exempt status. To assure that money directed toward such persons can be audited as charitable contributions, they should be funneled through a hospital, the Red Cross, Salvation Army, or other such institution that can redirect the aid to the individual. Just because a bank account has the ownership listed as the "John Doe Emergency Fund," it does not automatically mean that the fund is a bona fide charity.

**Electronic Meetings**    With today's easy electronic communications, polling of committee members between regularly scheduled annual meetings regarding emergency or short-notice donations can be done by conference calls, teleconferencing, or email. Although these methods are convenient in terms of time and expense, they seldom produce the same kinds of thoughtful results as do personal meetings. It may be stretching an analogy, but it's chilling to think what kinds of decisions members of Congress would reach if they operated electronically, without debate.

## Quarterly or Periodic Meetings

This is the most common pattern for meetings about corporate citizenship activities.

*Pros*    Management and board members often have quarterly meetings where information about profits is available for discussion. Because the members of management are already gathered, along with trusted staff, it's a good use of time and money to take advantage of being together for one purpose to address requests for your company's resources.

Companies tend to accumulate requests at a rate that has a loose relationship to their number of employees: roughly 6 to 8 requests per week per 100 employees. With 13 weeks per quarter, that means the committee could possibly have to consider as many as 104 requests at each meeting. Even if a staff person or committee member screens requests prior to the grants meeting, the committee will probably be reviewing between 25 and 50 proposals at a quarterly meeting. That still is a lot of reading! In practical terms, you can't let requests pile up any higher than that and still hope to give adequate consideration to each of them.

A good request will be written and submitted with ample time between submission and the time the money is needed or will be used. By meeting quarterly, the committee will be able to address most opportunities for non-emergency giving in a timely and deliberate manner.

*Cons*    If the members of the committee must be convened from substantial distances for the sole purpose of discussing and deciding upon the disposition of grants, the cost of this exercise (both in actual dollars and in person-hours) may exceed the benefit of the money distributed. Quarterly meetings work best when there is little geographic distance between members' work locations, or, as stated earlier, when they are already convened for other purposes.

When the number of requests piles up beyond the capacity of the committee members to fairly consider them, it may be wiser to choose another alternative.

## Rolling Schedule

*Pros*    One of the best parts of handling requests as they come in the door is that you don't miss an opportunity to give. The requests don't pile up. You know exactly how much money you have in your budget and can give all, none, or part of it immediately.

One part of the rolling schedule method that can be integrated into the rest of the options is to give one person the responsibility of reviewing requests as they come in and *rejecting* those that are clearly inappropriate for your company.

*Cons*   Most companies with more than 100 employees receive multiple requests weekly, if not daily. Therefore, handling them on an *ad hoc* basis will probably require the services of a staff person dedicated to this task. Unless that person has exceptional authorization in decision making, getting approval from a committee to issue grant checks will be constantly disruptive to people with other work to do. This is probably one of the reasons you've bought this book, just to avoid this situation.

Another negative of this method is the fact that you can easily and quickly exhaust your giving budget within the first week of your budgeting cycle, unless you put a cap on contributions for that period. In that case, it's quite likely that other, highly deserving projects will miss out on your generosity because the applications came in just after the last successful grant recipient got its check and the money ran out.

Handling requests in this way gives your company little opportunity for thoughtful, strategic grants. It is, however, one way to put a lid on requests: First come, first served.

## CHECKLIST

- ☐   Annual meeting
- ☐   Quarterly or periodic meeting
- ☐   Rolling schedule
- ☐   Executive prerogative
- ☐   Electronic meetings

## CHAPTER 7

# Budgeting and Financial Administration

The Number Two question I get asked in my consulting business is: How much is everyone else giving? When entering unknown territory, no one wants to be first.

In a little-known Biblical story, Moses was *not* the first of the Israelites to wade into the Red Sea while Pharaoh's army of horses and chariots was gaining upon them through the desert. According to legend, Moses stood on the high ground to rally the courage of his fearful followers. He needed someone to be brave, to be the trailblazer, because the Red Sea didn't open immediately.

That brave soul was Nachshon ben Amminadab. Nachshon waded in first to his ankles and called for the Children of Israel to follow. His words fell on deaf ears. He walked until he was in up to his waist. "Join me!" he cried. Still, no one came. The clouds were darkening above and the wind was fierce, whipping the waves.

Finally, Nachshon walked into the swirling sea until only his head above his chin was visible. His feet fought to keep him upright against the current that was now drawing in opposite directions to part the sea, following the will of a power from the heavens. The Children of Israel saw Nachshon's courageous stand and gasped as the Red Sea divided at his last exhortation for them to follow him. And follow him they did, into freedom.

Giving when your company has never given before need not be such a fearful, dramatic, or emotional experience as leaping into the Red Sea. But you must take a leap of faith at some point and commit to getting your feet wet before you are comfortable with the process and are walking on a dry, clear path.

## PERCENTAGE GIVING

You're still wondering, though, "How much *does* everyone else give?" Of those businesses that give to charity, the national average has hovered around 1.2 percent of pretax profits for nearly two decades. That 1.2 percent is not just cash; it includes cash (including stocks), products and services, and the value of hours volunteered by employees on company time. There are still thousands of businesses that give nothing.

Like the old television commercial about prunes—"Is three enough; is six too many?"—you may ask if 1.2 percent is the right formula for *your* company. It may well be enough, depending on what you want to accomplish through your giving.

In many of the larger U.S. cities, the Chamber of Commerce sponsors a "Two Percent Club." Some Chambers may even have members of a "Five Percent Club"; they may be called "The Keystone Program" or something similar. Their goals are all the same: to recognize and thank businesses that give between 2 and 5 percent of pretax profits to charity.

The first Keystone Program was founded in 1976, with commitments from 23 Minnesota companies to give at least 2 percent of their pretax earnings to address community needs. Their goal was simply to sustain the community's heritage of generosity and community spirit to maintain a high quality of life.[1]

In 1976, these 23 companies included H.G. Fuller, the industrial glues and solvents giant; equipment manufacturer Graco; the Carlson Companies, which own the Radisson Hotel chain; and the predecessors to the Target Corporation and Wells Fargo Bank Minnesota. Unquestionably, these are major players in local economies and even the national economy. Was the Keystone Program destined to be another old-boys' club for the business elite? By no means. In 2002, 51 percent of the Minnesota Keystone Program members were companies with fewer than 75 employees (see Exhibit 7.1).

Is this program just for public companies with high-profile images to maintain? No again. More than three-quarters of the members are privately held companies or EOCs.

The accounting system for these programs takes into consideration that many mid-market and small companies are owned by one or two individuals. In these cases, donations made by the business owners out of their personal checkbooks also can be counted in the 2 percent equation. Although strategic philanthropy in the context of corporate citizenship excludes donations to the business owner's house of worship, Keystone Programs recognize that personal and business giving cannot be easily separated in the case of sole proprietorships. In the end, the goal of such a program is to foster philanthropy in any form.

Still, the greatest potential for new members remains in the mid-market and small business groups. Why haven't they joined Keystone in the numbers that equal their real representation in the business sector? Perhaps it is that the owners don't understand the lesson that Keystone members have learned: *Doing good for the community is good for business.* Remember, according to O'Connell, companies receiving the Ad Council's Public Service Award showed annual growth in profits of 11 percent compounded over 30 years, significantly outpacing the GNP for the same period.

There is often a "benefit of membership" available to Keystone members. Numerous member companies have policies that state a preference for doing business with other

EXHIBIT 7.1    MINNESOTA KEYSTONE PROGRAM
2001 PARTICIPANT SUMMARY

The Keystone Program members commit to give either 2 or 5 percent of pretax profits to charity. That makes it easy to budget for charitable contributions.

| Giving Levels | # | % |
|---|---|---|
| Five percent (5+%) | 140 | 61% |
| Two percent (2–4.9%) | 87 | 38% |
| Pledge to reach 2% in 3 years | 4 | 1% |
| **Industry Sector** | | |
| Business/Professional Services | 90 | 39% |
| Finance/Insurance | 49 | 21% |
| Manufacturing/Distribution | 42 | 18% |
| Real Estate/Construction | 14 | 7% |
| Retail/Personal | 10 | 5% |
| Publishing/Media | 13 | 6% |
| Hospitality/Entertainment | 6 | 2% |
| Nonprofit/Education | 3 | 1% |
| Utilities/Transportation | 4 | 1% |
| **Company Size** | | |
| Less than 75 employees | 118 | 51% |
| 76–499 employees | 59 | 26% |
| 500–1,999 employees | 28 | 12% |
| 2,000–4,999 employees | 9 | 4% |
| More than 5,000 employees | 17 | 7% |
| **Organization Ownership** | | |
| EOC | 60 | 26% |
| Privately held | 136 | 59% |
| Publicly held | 28 | 12% |
| Other | 7 | 3% |

*Source:* "The Business of Giving Back: 2002 Survey of Business Giving and Community Involvement," prepared by Wilder Research Center, St. Paul, MN, for Building Business Investment in Community, a statewide Minnesota Keystone Program, Minneapolis Regional Chamber of Commerce.

members. Dozens of smaller businesses must vie for contracts with Keystone members, such as General Mills, that demonstrate an affinity for other good corporate citizens.

If one of your goals in giving is to be counted among the businesses that are considered the best corporate citizens in America, then 2 percent is a target you should set for yourself.

Certainly, there are many businesses that give 2 and 5 percent and even more without subscribing to or joining this kind of program. They often want to remain anonymous. They do it for other reasons that you and I will never know. Too often they do it without realizing what they're doing. They give without a budget for giving and end up nickel and dimeing (or shall we say $50-ing and $100-ing) themselves into a shaky bottom line.

## SET DOLLAR AMOUNT

Giving a percentage may not be the way you want to go, for whatever reason you choose. In that case, you may want to set a target dollar amount in your company's budget (see Exhibit 7.2).

### Budgeting Pros and Cons

Setting aside a specific amount for giving in any given year has distinct advantages. First, it allows you to decide how much to give, as you allocate all other foreseeable expenditures during your budgeting process. Second, because the money is allocated at the beginning of the fiscal year, there is no guessing as to what the dollar amount of a percentage of profits will be.

Therein may lie a problem. When you set aside a distinct budget for giving and business goes into a downturn, such as too many companies have experienced in the beginning of

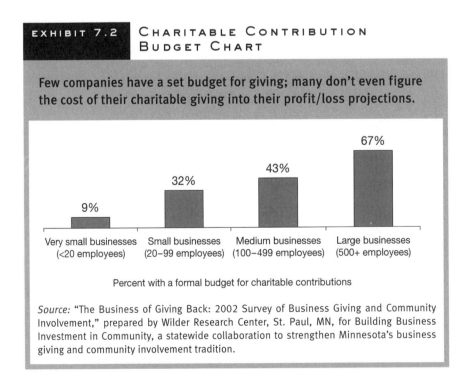

**EXHIBIT 7.2**    CHARITABLE CONTRIBUTION BUDGET CHART

Few companies have a set budget for giving; many don't even figure the cost of their charitable giving into their profit/loss projections.

Percent with a formal budget for charitable contributions

- Very small businesses (<20 employees): 9%
- Small businesses (20–99 employees): 32%
- Medium businesses (100–499 employees): 43%
- Large businesses (500+ employees): 67%

*Source:* "The Business of Giving Back: 2002 Survey of Business Giving and Community Involvement," prepared by Wilder Research Center, St. Paul, MN, for Building Business Investment in Community, a statewide collaboration to strengthen Minnesota's business giving and community involvement tradition.

this century, the temptation to dip into your charitable budget can be strong. Although cutting back on charitable donations is by no means illegal or unethical, it may have detrimental effects on what we discussed in the introduction to this book: competitive context.

How can you maintain a relatively stable level of giving and avoid the temptation to nibble away at your company's contributions budget? The most common way is to set up a company foundation.

## CORPORATE FOUNDATIONS AND DONOR-ADVISED FUNDS

Most of the largest foundations in the United States have their roots, directly or indirectly, in business. Some, like Target or Kellogg, bear the name of the company that established them and still depend heavily on donations from the corporate parent or on the performance of that company's stock, which generally constitutes a substantial portion of the foundation's endowment. Others, like the Ford Foundation, have cut almost all of the bonds that once tied them to the parent company.

You don't need to be a multinational conglomerate to set up a corporate foundation. In reality, you don't even need to set up a separate foundation to function as one. Let's examine some of your options.

### Private Foundation

There's a lot of prestige involved in setting up a private foundation. A private foundation, usually endowed with a generous portion of company stock, says that your company has reached a stage of strength and stability that allows the owners to institutionalize their philanthropy. Their confidence in the company's success is so great that they are comfortable in forfeiting exclusive control over these assets to the foundation trustees.

The big corporate foundations, like Target and Eli Lilly, usually have broad programs addressing causes as diverse as the arts and health care. Their huge endowments allow them that leverage.

Smaller company foundations may focus very closely on something that they can afford and that can have very specific paybacks for the company. The B.H. Chesley Foundation in Minnesota exclusively funds scholarships for automotive mechanic students in local trade schools. Not surprisingly, the B.H. Chesley Foundation is tied to the Chesley Truck Company. The Chesley Foundation cannot specify or coerce scholarship winners to work for the company, but it can still pave the way for young mechanics to take the road to employment with Chesley.

A big advantage in having a private foundation is that you, as a trustee, can maintain control over its investment portfolio, which may include a major chunk of your company's stock. Decisions regarding the foundation's investment policy are vital if you want to maintain a steady or growing budget for corporate contributions. The contrasting investment policies of the two private foundations established by the founders of the Hewlett-Packard Corporation is a classic example:

- *The Packard Foundation adhered to the wishes of founder David Packard and maintained its endowment invested nearly entirely in HP stock. In the high times of the 1990s, the Packard Foundation was one of the top ten foundations in the country. When the dotcom bubble burst, so did the Packard Foundation's endowment and consequent capacity to give.*

- *The Hewlett Foundation, in contrast, played the "poor stepsister" role during the 1990s, but suffered not nearly as severely as did the Packard Foundation when the economy turned sharply downward. The trustees diversified the foundation's portfolio immediately each time Bill Hewlett donated HP stock to it. The Hewlett Foundation still holds 20 percent of its endowment in HP stock, but the wise investment policy of the trustees has allowed the foundation to maintain a steady level of philanthropy.*

An interesting variation on this strategy was created by Otto Bremer, founder of the Bremer Banks in Minnesota and the Otto Bremer Foundation. He turned the tables on the corporate profit model and left all the shares of his bank corporation to his foundation. All profits from the Bremer Banks go to the Otto Bremer Foundation and are granted to worthy nonprofits in Bremer Bank communities. Otto Bremer understood competitive context! Bremer Banks are some of the most successful and trusted in the country—which is saying a lot at a time when bank and corporate executives are being scrutinized for exorbitant salaries and questionable ethical conduct.

Of course, there's also a lot of expense in setting up a private foundation. Depending on the sophistication of the institution, drawing up the legal documents and filing tax forms can cost as much as $10,000. If you intend to endow your company foundation with $3 million, then this is a trivial amount. However, few mid-market businesses are ready to make a $3 million commitment up front. Few mid-market companies employ a staff attorney; even if they do, that person may or may not be able to draw up the legal instruments for a foundation. You may also find that this kind of activity is not covered by your contractual retainer to the law firm that handles your company's other legal needs.

Your company may choose to make annual gifts to the company foundation, particularly in the early years of operation, rather than making large donations for an endowment. This pass-through method of giving and granting allows the trustees to take a little more time in deciding how to spend the money for charity, because foundations are required to give away only 5 percent of their assets in any one year.

To further explore what corporate foundations do and learn what steps you should take to set one up, contact the National Council on Foundations or the local affiliate office of the Council of Regional Grantmakers.

## Donor-Advised Funds

Setting up a donor-advised fund at a community foundation, one of the national service foundations, or with one of the foundations established by investment firms is another good choice if you want to maintain that dollar-certain level of giving. The advantages of donor-advised funds are that they:

- Can be set up with relatively small initial donations.

- Have very small administrative charges and provide a certain level of administrative support.

- Generally have good investment policies to safeguard your endowment.

Some disadvantages are that they:

- Do not allow you to manage the investment of your endowment.

- Are not perpetual. Generally, after a certain number of years, any money in the endowment reverts to the umbrella organization for its administrative costs or for projects of *its* choice, which may not be *your* choice.

With a well-planned donor-advised fund, the only differences between it and a private foundation are the management of the investments, the name of the entity filing the tax forms, and the signature on the bottom of the check written to charity. You and those you designate as trustees of the company fund still make the decisions about how the money is given away. *You* direct the umbrella foundation as to how to disburse the money.

To make a donor-advised fund work for you and your company, you must treat the program planning and certain parts of your administration, such as proposal review, the same way you would if you had created an independent foundation. Part of that planning takes us back to where this chapter starts: deciding how much you want to give.

## OTHER PARTS OF THE EQUATION

Whether you decide to set a percent or a fixed dollar amount as your giving goal, you still must figure out what constitutes the components of your company's giving. If you are budgeting:

- Should charitable donations come directly from profits, or should they be built into the budgets of various departments?

- Should each department have the same amount or percent of budget allocated for donations, or should there be variation according to the size of the department, revenues generated by that division, and so on?

- Will donations made strictly from company profits directly to charities be counted toward the total?

- Should contributions given through employee drives, such as United Way, count as well? That is money that they have *earned* on the job and for which individual employees may not even receive separate receipts. Yet, it will be the company that will most likely receive recognition from the charity.

- Will you count donations made from the private checkbooks of owners as part of the philanthropic goal?

When you have made these decisions, then you're ready to build the figures into your profit/loss projections and move on to the next issue in planning.

## CHECKLIST

### *Structure*

- ☐ Company foundation
- ☐ Endowment
- ☐ Pass-through
- ☐ Donor-advised fund
- ☐ From pretax profits

### *Budgeting*

- ☐ Specific dollar amount annually
- ☐ Percentage of profits
- ☐ Company-wide pool
- ☐ Allocation to department/unit
- ☐ By size
- ☐ By revenue
- ☐ By profit
    - ☐ Include owner's private donations in pool
    - ☐ Include employee donations in total

# 8

# Identify Internal Areas for Impact

Your company has a strategic plan that encompasses all parts of your operations. Parts of the plan call for growth or expansion: You want to roll out a new product. You want to increase sales of existing products in existing markets. You want to cut down on employee turnover. You want to open sales or operations in a new community. The kinds of causes your company supports should relate to its strategic business priorities. Let's look at some case studies.

## STOPPING EMPLOYEE TURNOVER

I had a client whose family-owned company manufactured portable displays for education and industrial trade shows. The company employed only a few people with highly technical skills. The majority of its employees were semi-skilled workers involved in manufacturing and assembly. Most of them lived close to the plant, located in a blue-collar suburb.

The company had a problem with employee turnover. With so many manufacturers in the area, it was easy for the blue-collar workers to go job-hopping if an opportunity arose for more interesting work or slightly better pay. It cost the company lots of money to continuously recruit and train new employees. They needed to stop the turnover.

Differences in benefits, pay, and work conditions between my client and his neighbors were minimal. If one offered better benefits, the other offered a higher hourly wage. How could my client entice his employees to stay around?

The company's first attempt at using corporate citizenship to build esprit de corps among coworkers, and consequent loyalty to the company, was only a partial success. Management signed up for volunteers to build a Habitat for Humanity house. Although this seemed like a good idea, as many of the workers had construction skills, it turned out to be less than completely successful, because many of the employees wanted to do something *other* than construction on their time off. Participation was less than it could have been.

The company owners looked again at their workers. Which workers seemed to be moving the most, looking for the best deal? It turned out that the most mobile workers were those with children approaching college age. The workers were trying to get as much saved for their kids' education as possible. This, then, was the clue the owners needed.

They decided to offer college scholarships for the children of employees with more than five years of tenure with the company. Because the majority of workers lived in two or three nearby school districts, the schools could be the nonprofit fiduciary for the scholarship program, ensuring a tax deduction for the company.

The company awards the scholarship every year at the company picnic. There's no describing the pride displayed by the proud employee-parents when the young scholars are introduced to the entire company and their families. The scholarship winners and the parents appear in the company newsletter, in some of the printed materials used for promoting the company's products (especially to their educational clients), and in recruiting literature. You can bet that the worker will want to stay with the company long after the student has graduated!

## LAUNCHING NEW PRODUCTS

If your company manufactures widget components for larger widget manufacturers and distributors, then it might not be feasible to use corporate citizenship activities to launch a new product. You might want to concentrate on other parts of your strategic plan and see where giving fits it best.

If, however, you manufacture, sell, or distribute consumer products, there are dozens of creative ways to tie in what you want to sell with charity. When Select Comfort started its sales and marketing, theirs was a totally new product. There are dozens of mattress companies in competition, but Select Comfort's Sleep Number bed was a new technology. Too many consumers, though, think that new is scary and they are reluctant to make such a major purchase from an unknown.

Select Comfort has some very humorous and effective television ads to market its products. But this kind of marketing is unquestionably expensive and is not targetted at people who may have compelling reasons to buy a Sleep Number bed—other than that their spouse tosses and turns a lot during the night. Select Comfort's product research team learned that persons with mobility problems, such as paraplegics or comatose patients, developed virtually no bed sores if they slept on properly adjusted Sleep Number beds. Select Comfort could imagine huge hospital and nursing home supply contracts. But there's another way into that market: the families of patients who must care for those patients at home.

How could Select Comfort introduce these people to its product and make a strong enough impression to convince them to buy? Executives from Select Comfort approached the managers of the local Ronald McDonald House.

Ronald McDonald Houses are found in close proximity to major research hospitals around the country. They exist to house the parents (and often additional family members) of children who are undergoing long-term treatment and therapy for life-threatening conditions. They need a lot of beds. And they need beds that will allow people with a *lot* on their minds to get some truly restful sleep.

Many of the children being treated also have severe short- or long-term mobility problems. They and their parents will have good experiences on the Sleep Number beds at Ronald McDonald Houses and will probably learn about the research results of the beds' benefits for their children. They can easily put one and one together, which adds up to a Sleep Number bed in at least one bedroom, once they bring the little tyke home.

Ronald McDonald Houses win: They get free mattresses. The families win: They get a product that addresses a specialized need. Select Comfort wins in two ways: The company gets a tax deduction for the mattresses given to the Ronald McDonald Houses, and it gets a sale or sales to the family. Select Comfort doesn't advertise its good citizenship with Ronald McDonald Houses. However, it allows the charity to acknowledge and publicize Select Comfort's generosity among its donors. That's called free advertising with another market.

## Expanding Sales of Existing Products

Once again, widget component manufacturers may want to jump over this section. One of the oldest ways to expand sales of existing products is to offer coupons or other premiums to entice consumers to purchase your product. The consumer has two possible motivations to purchase the product this way: save money or get a bonus.

In the infancy of cause-related marketing back in the 1980s, I was working for CARE, the international aid and development organization—the original "CARE Package" people. We were approached by one of the large food manufacturers. They had been donating tons of unsalable but perfectly edible food to CARE for years, and knew that the organization had a sterling reputation. They also knew that CARE had one of the largest donor lists in the country.

This manufacturer's marketing department had come up with a campaign whereby CARE would receive a certain small donation for every coupon returned for the company's products. In other words, buying food for your family would translate into buying food for a hungry family in the Third World.

CARE agreed to cooperate on the project, but because we'd never done anything like this before, we were worried that we'd never be able to reach the $100,000 cap that the company put on the campaign. The company's ad stated that every coupon returned meant money for CARE, but we couldn't be sure that sufficient numbers of new consumers would be motivated to buy or that existing consumers would buy more just because of the CARE connection.

We swung into action. We sent out direct-mail letters to all of our donors, alerting them to the promotion. Articles appeared in our newsletters about it. Public service ads mentioned the campaign. We felt good about promoting the company's products, not just because it would bring us new money, but also because we already had a positive relationship with the company from its many years of product donations.

The response was fantastic. The general public recognized CARE's name, and it's highly likely that some consumers bought the products because it was an easy way to support a worthy cause. Our donors wrote in and told us how they cut coupons from the newspapers of their friends and relatives to use when buying the product, so that CARE could get just that much more.

In the end, we far exceeded the original $100,000 cap, and the company ended up making good on every coupon. They sold a *lot* of product, and I can imagine that many of those who bought became repeat customers.

You don't have to be a multinational food company to follow this example. Your coffee house is in the food business. You may already donate your end-of-the-day baked products to a local homeless shelter. But you can also offer a donation to the shelter to your customers for every tenth cup of coffee they buy. It's easy to keep track. Each time they turn in their "current cup" card, it means another donation to the shelter. All those volunteers at the shelter will learn about your program and you may just gain some new regulars from among their ranks.

## Lowering Payroll Costs

Widget component manufacturers—this is for *you!* Competition in the widget component business is fierce. The widget corporation you supply is constantly threatening to switch suppliers to keep the cost of *its* product competitive.

What can you do? You can try to get more productivity out of your current workforce. You can cut the workforce and add hours for those who remain. That may not save money in the end, if overtime turns out to be excessive and you end up losing the good workers you have due to stress. Outsourcing is not an option. Your customer outsources to *you*.

Have you thought of hiring the handicapped? Most companies don't think of this as a corporate citizenship activity, but many of the sources that supply qualified handicapped workers are nonprofit organizations.

There are generally two ways that these organizations can meet your needs: in-house or outsourcing. In either case, your costs are, to a greater or lesser degree, underwritten by the nonprofit that provides the workers.

Businesses are often reluctant to hire persons with disabilities because they have various questions and reservations: If it hires a person in a wheelchair, what kind of physical accommodations will the company have to make regarding transportation and work-space? Will the changes prove to be costly? How much extra supervision will a develop-mentally disabled worker need to get the job done right?

Businesses that hire the handicapped or use sheltered workshop services do not receive charitable deductions for doing so. But they do get good workers, or keep costs down, and with those advantages they might want to make a donation to the charity that provides the service. We'll be looking at this more closely from a different angle in Chapter 9.

## IMPROVING THE COMPANY'S IMAGE OR RAISING ITS PROFILE

The earlier example of CARE and the food company was one instance of cause-related marketing. We deal with this subject further in Chapter 10, which has great appeal for marketing directors, but we must at least touch on it here.

A survey conducted in 2000 by Cone, Inc. and Roper-Starch Worldwide, and reported in the *Chronicle of Philanthropy,* revealed that teenagers react highly favorably to compa-nies that demonstrate support for charitable causes. The report showed that "[w]hen price and quality are the same, 9 out of 10 teenagers said they would switch brands to one associated with a cause they care about."[1] And, as those engaged in the ongoing furor over Hollywood's marketing to youngsters point out, teens have deep pockets in those baggy jeans.

Cause-related marketing and cause branding are not new. Paul Newman's many food products have been on the market for years and state clearly on the label that the profits go to charity. Some of the charities are ones that Newman himself founded, such as Camp Hole-in-the-Wall for underprivileged children.

We've already learned some things about Ronald McDonald Houses. Although anyone, including your business, can support the Ronald McDonald Houses, it's clear that their primary funding source is branded with the creator of the eponymous "spokes-man"—the McDonald's Corporation.

The Cone/Roper survey shows the increasing popularity and success of cause-related marketing: From 1993 through 1998, cause-related related marketing gained 8 per-centage points as an accepted business practice.

Cause-related marketing helps bring your company visibility in any number of ways. You may be recognized by your industry for your citizenship, or by such notable orga-nizations as your local chapter of the Association of Fundraising Professionals.

Whether selling video games to pubescent boys or computer chips to a multinational corporation, cause-related marketing should be part of every company's business plan. Whether you as a business owner administer the plan yourself, or run it out of your mar-keting, community affairs, or human resources department, it can be one of the key strategies to raise your company's visibility, credibility, and profitability. Cause-related marketing is powerful, it's ethical, and it works.

## CHECKLIST

- ❑ Stop employee turnover
- ❑ Attract new employees
- ❑ Launch new products and services
- ❑ Expand sales of existing products and services
- ❑ Attract new customers
- ❑ Attract customers from competitors
- ❑ Lower payroll costs
- ❑ Improve image and raise profile of company or product

## CHAPTER 9

# Ways of Giving

For most unsophisticated donors, there are just two ways to give: cash or check. Many businesses are familiar with gifts of products or services as well. Volunteering is a gift of time, either from the company owner or from your employees—on or off the job, with the company's blessing or without it. Time has a cash value.

In this section, we will look at the myriad number of ways of giving. Though the list here is long, it is far from exhaustive. The options can multiply if your business is privately held, particularly if it is held by an individual or an individual family. For individual giving, you should consult with an attorney, accountant, or financial planner about the various giving vehicles you can create that relate to your business, and even play a role in business succession into the next generation.

## GIFTS OF CASH OR CASH EQUIVALENT

On his website, the Attorney General of the State of Minnesota (*www.ag.state.mn.us*) warns all donors: *Don't give cash.* He means greenbacks, folding money. No matter how well-intentioned the staff of a nonprofit may be, the temptation to pocket cash when no one is looking can be overwhelming. When you give cash, unless you receive a receipt on the spot, you may be out of luck in claiming a deduction if you don't have a paper trail to prove your generosity.

Writing a check is most common. You have proof in your checkbook that the donation was made, and we hope that you will get a receipt confirming the fact that the charity received and deposited it. When you write the check, though, are you making sure that your company is getting the maximum financial leverage out of your donation?

## EQUAL OPPORTUNITY GIVING

The way that most small businesses operate their charitable donations is "come one, come all" or "first come, first served." In other words, anyone who asks gets as much as they ask for as long as the money lasts. Unfortunately, that's what put you in the situation you're facing now and why you're reading this book to learn some alternatives.

Equal opportunity giving is the simplest variation on the "first come, first served" method, but it can still give you more control over your giving. First, set aside a budget for giving. Make it generous: at least as much as you gave last year (if you have an idea of how much that was). Next, look at the number of checks you wrote to charity last year and increase the amount somewhat. Divide the budgeted dollars by the number of checks you are willing to write. That will be your target donation level. Make a photocopied statement to give to all donation seekers, explaining that your company has a policy of giving $X to all worthy charities—take it or leave it.

Most will take it. That leaves you with more time to dedicate to business. It doesn't leave you with a great public image, but you've met what you consider to be your obligations.

## United Way and Other Federated Charities

If your company cannot afford the luxury of a paid employee dedicated or partly dedicated to administering a corporate citizenship program, participating in a federated charity program may be for you. These programs are also excellent for companies that are not yet profitable but want to give back to the community in some way.

That way is through the payroll deductions and volunteer, on-premises fundraising activities of employees. Depending on your community and the size of the resources of the federated charity, its staff may run all the fundraising activities for you. Your company doesn't have to make its own separate donation, but it is still recognized as a sponsor, which is important in building a reputation in the local business community.

## Matching and Challenge Grants

### Matching Grants

Anyone who listens to public radio is familiar with the pledge-drive gimmick called the *matching grant*. "For the next 15 minutes, every donation will be matched on a 2:1 basis by the Joe Schmoe Foundation," the program host announces. The previously silent phones start ringing off the hook (which shows that your author has not yet reached a state of wireless telecommunication in her imagery). Those listeners want to get the biggest bang for their donation buck, so they *wait* to make their pledges until there is a match opportunity.

In business, it's common for a company to match the contributions to charity made by its employees. What is the advantage to the company in matching? First and foremost is employee loyalty. The employee sees that the company cares about what *she* cares about and that it supports her interests and passions. An additional perceived or real benefit for the employee is that the employee is able to stretch his income. For community-minded but low-wage workers who don't itemize charitable contributions on their tax returns, this means cash back into their pockets.

There are variations within this category.

- *Simple Matches.* The management offers to match the donations of its employees on a 1:1, 2:1, or other basis for any charity of the employee's choice. There may be some minor restrictions on eligibility, such as donations for churches or politically sensitive issues.

- *Unequal Matches.* These encourage employees to give to certain charities by offering a more favorable match. The company may have a "charity of the month" or other special program. If the employee supports *that* charity, the match will be, say, 2:1. If it's for another, the match may be only 1:2.

## Challenge Grants

Challenge grants are a great way to get the biggest bang for your buck *and* build capacity within the charity.

K Mart may be but a shadow of its former retail-giant self, but the Kresge Foundation that bears the name of the original company is still a major player in the philanthropy world. The Kresge Foundation distinguishes itself by issuing challenge grants only: Kresge will give 50 percent of the proposed project costs if the charity can find other donors to pay the rest of the bill.

In this way, Kresge shares the risk of the project. It also assures that the charity doesn't depend too heavily on one source of giving. When charities depend too strongly on an "angel investor" or "sugar daddy" donor, they run the risk of program or organizational failure when that lone source of support is withdrawn.

Issuing a challenge grant gives your donation both muscle and prestige. It also means that you'll be giving a large donation. Your company must be willing and able to assume the financial responsibility involved and accept the prestige associated with challenge granting.

## LEAD GIFTS

Your company might want to distinguish itself by being a lead giver. Do you remember Nachshon ben Amminadab? He had the courage to go first.

When charities are going for big dollars, particularly capital or endowment campaigns, they always need a major gift to get the show on the road. I had a client who decided to go this route for some very interesting reasons:

- He knew he'd be making a real difference in the success of the campaign.

- If he only gave major gifts to kick off big campaigns, he could turn down all the bothersome requests for $25 or to buy tables at banquets. "Come back to me when you've got a *really* big project," he'd tell them. If they were serious about doing a meaningful, long-term program, they'd be back and he'd be glad to consider a major gift. But only a few came back, and his time and money were used very effectively as a result.

## Over-the-Top Gifts

In contrast, there is the complement to the lead gift: making the final donation that puts a campaign "over the top." Major charitable campaigns can drag on for years, or may even be unsuccessful because they lack the large gift that will get them to their goal. When the campaign involves a challenge grant, this can be particularly devastating, as a challenge grant is usually not paid until all other pledges are in place.

Your company can distinguish itself and make a difference by giving through this method. You may want to put some qualifiers on your participation: You will give only when the charity is within a particular dollar amount or percentage of its fundraising goal. For example, if the campaign is for $1 million, you might want to restrict your giving to the last $50,000 or less. A big advantage of this method is the level of donor recognition you are sure to get for being such a hero and saving the campaign!

## Tributes and Awards

Turning your corporate citizenship program into an award competition has advantages both for the charity and for your company. In an award competition, as opposed to a grants program, the charity (or potential scholarship winner) can be nominated by a third party, as well as charities that nominate themselves. Small groups that are doing exceptional work, but that don't have enough staff of their own to go through the screening process, may find that someone else, such as a politician, is doing the work for them. When done well, an award program can bring substantial publicity to both the giver and the receiver.

If your company decides to do awards, there are two ways of handling it financially. You can make one or two awards per year, give an impressive plaque or statue to the winners, and make the financial prize substantial. This gives tremendous prestige to both the prize and the winners. You make a big impact with a small audience.

The alternative is to award inexpensive certificates and smaller checks to a larger group of worthy candidates. This approach can gain your company a different kind of visibility: a smaller impact with a bigger market. Awards programs usually generate less paperwork for your committee. Once a group has won an award, it is unlikely to apply for the award again in the near future, in contrast to nonprofits that seek grants year after year.

Nonprofits that win prestigious awards find that their fundraising ability is enhanced with other prospective donors. Nothing succeeds like success.

## Donation of Products and Services

Businesses of all sizes are asked for donations of products and services. An example that I use in some of my seminars is from the cartoon series *For Better or For Worse* by Lynn Johnston (see Exhibit 9.1).

Elly and her assistant are straightening the shelves in their tiny children's book and toy store. In the first panel, a patron comes in requesting a donation to thank hospital volunteers, and Elly offers a set of books. In the second panel, she gives a teddy bear for a charity silent auction. She responds generously to the tyke in the third panel who asks for a prize for the junior baseball league. In the final panel, Elly's assistant remarks, "I like the way you support all the non-profit organizations"—to which she responds, "Yes . . . we're about as non-profit as you get!"

Giving products is causing Elly some problems. They are eating away at her good inventory and diminishing her slim profit margin.

For other companies, though, giving products can solve a big problem. Did you ever wonder what happened to those baby tee-shirts you returned to Target after you opened the package and discovered that the baby had outgrown that size a month ago? Certainly, Target doesn't receive enough of this kind of return to warrant the cost of repackaging them and adding them back into stock.

**EXHIBIT 9.1**  The Pain of Slow Drain

Small businesses have a difficult time saying no to people who are not just customers, but also friends and neighbors. Even these people realize that there are limits to what you can do when they ask, and will accept that half a loaf is better than none when you present your guidelines to them.

**For Better or For Worse** *by Lynn Johnston*

*Source:* Lynn Johnston Productions/United Features Syndicate, Inc.

Instead, those open packages are donated to Goodwill Industries. Needy families who can't afford to shop even at Target can get first-quality, unused merchandise at super-bargain prices by shopping at Goodwill. Goodwill, in turn, uses the funds for its job training and supported workshops for the handicapped.

Elly has to learn to give strategically. I'm not here to tell Elly precisely how to give, but she might be well served by thinking a bit more strategically when she gives away books. Maybe becoming a bigger patron of the Friends of the Library would give her greater visibility among a market of people who truly appreciate books.

When giving products, be sure that your accountant takes the appropriate tax deduction, depending on the kind of inventory you donate. The IRS has clear rules on the amount that can be written off.

For very small business owners, giving like Elly can be tricky and not very cost-effective. Let's take the stuffed animal that she is donating for a raffle. Elly wants to sell the toy for $16.95, and it may fetch more than that in the sale of tickets to even one donor. But Elly can only take the wholesale cost of the toy as her tax deduction. For the self-employed artist who shows and sells her own art, the write-off is even smaller: She can deduct only the cost of her materials when she gives a sculpture to the charity silent auction committee. It's another occupational hazard of the proverbial starving artist! In these cases, the business owner may be better off making a cash donation.

## Hiring the Handicapped

This does not mean that you will be hiring people with disabilities and putting them on your payroll, although this is certainly appropriate when qualified candidates apply for a job with your company and you can accommodate them under the Americans with Disabilities Act. What we are talking about here are nonprofit organizations that offer businesses a number of benefits by underwriting employment opportunities for persons with physical or mental handicaps.

People with disabilities often have skills that command market-rate salaries of great value to your company. What prevents them from working alongside your regular employees may be something as simple as transportation. You can't afford, on your own, to provide a van for one employee like this to come to work. But if others in your industrial park join you in working with a nonprofit to hire these grateful workers, a small donation to the charity will pay for the van and driver to bring them to the job on time and reliably.

If you do hire persons with disabilities to work on your payroll, often there are government programs that will subsidize their salaries. These vary from state to state.

An associate of mine who works for a nonprofit that provides advocacy and transportation for developmentally disabled adults described a situation that demonstrates the importance of these jobs to the disabled and the value such jobs have for their families. About a dozen clients had been working on site for a major fast-food chain for several years, washing trays. The corporation changed its policy so that all employees had to be able to carry out all jobs. Clearly, this was beyond the abilities of the tray washers, and they were all let go.

Their families were up in arms. They organized a boycott of the restaurants in question. They went to the local press. The boycott worked for quite a while, but given the lopsided power balance between the families and the corporation, the brouhaha eventually died down. Still, those boycotters will never darken the doorways of those restaurants again, and neither will many of their friends. If you are hiring the handicapped, you make a moral commitment as much as a financial one.

If you cannot accommodate the disabled on your premises, there are different ways to hire them. Other charities provide sheltered workshops for the handicapped to provide services such as assembly or mailing, or even customer service in call centers. Rather than make a donation to that organization, you may decide to hire its sponsored workers for projects. Do you remember the highest step on the ladder of charity? It's giving a person a job so that he or she no longer needs charity.

## Buying Products and Services from Nonprofits

Buying Girl Scout cookies is part of American culture, but they are not necessarily the kind of refreshments you want to have on the table during breaks at your board meeting. One Twin Cities nonprofit does double duty in its programming and financing by baking and selling premium cookies. The charity targets at-risk inner-city teens. Under adult supervision, the teens conduct all the operations of a bakery, from purchasing ingredients and equipment, to baking, to sales and delivery, then on into accounting. Profits are used to give participants scholarships for other learning experiences for future careers. Your board eats fabulous cookies and the kids live better lives.

Another example is frequently seen at the end of the year. Your receptionist dreads this season. Your weight-conscious front-desk receptionist is deluged with "holiday gifts" from every sales rep who has walked in the door since January. The rep has a basket of candy for the receptionist and maybe a bottle of wine for you. The gift is not appreciated and often isn't used in the way it's meant to be. Is *your* company also throwing its money away on unappreciated gifts?

Many charities have tribute cards; often they print special cards for the holiday season. The wording is pretty standard no matter what the charity: "Yourtown Community Fund has received a generous gift in your name from Your Company." It may have some information about the charity on the card. It's a great gift. One size fits all, the color is always right, and it's not fattening. You kill three birds with one stone by making a thoughtful gift to a valued client, making a tax-deductible donation to a worthy cause, and demonstrating the true meaning of the season at the same time.

## Scholarships

Scholarships are one of the most popular forms of corporate citizenship. Scholarships are different than reimbursing your employees for continuing education that directly relates to their job performance. When we speak of scholarships, we mean one of two kinds: employee-related or non-employee-related.

### Employee-Related

These scholarships are generally set up by the company to benefit children or other family members of employees. Often they are viewed as an additional employment benefit.

There are a couple of ways to set up these scholarships to assure the tax deductibility of the financial contribution from your company.

1. If your company draws its employees nearly exclusively from one school district, you can donate the money to the district and allow it to select winners according to criteria that you will set forth in a memorandum of agreement. (See samples in Appendix C.)

2. If your company draws employees from a broader geographic area, you may want to set up a fund with a community foundation, the Scholarship America,[1] or another umbrella foundation, or start your own company foundation for this purpose. The scholarships, again, will be awarded by the trustees of that institution according to the memorandum of agreement you will create.

The memorandum of agreement, of course, will spell out that the applicant/candidate must be related to a person employed by your company. It may also dictate certain standards to be met by the candidates (e.g., a particular grade-point average), or attendance at a college or institution that meets certain criteria (e.g., degree-granting institution rather than a trade school). It will also state whether a representative of your company will be on the committee that makes the selections.

To meet the requirements of the Internal Revenue Service for tax deductibility, if your company is giving the money to a school board, for instance, your representative *can* be involved in the selection, but it *cannot* have majority influence in selecting scholarship winners.

### Non-Employee-Related

In contrast, if you establish a company foundation, it would be possible for all of the trustees to be company employees. You may want to have this kind of control if you are giving scholarships to young people who are not related to your employees, as you will know less about them to start with.

Offering scholarships to people who are not connected to your company accomplishes several goals:

- When properly structured, these kinds of scholarships create a pipeline for possible new employees for your company. If your company manufactures widgets and you sponsor a scholarship in the widget-technology program at your local college, it can create a greater awareness of your company as a possible employer to the scholar. Of course, if the student can't wait to get out of your one-horse town and see the wide world, there's no way you can ethically keep him from picking up and using his valuable talents to work for your competition in another part of the country.

- It improves that all-important competitive context for your community and your industry.

Both kinds of scholarship models are wonderful tools for building employee morale. We'll discuss how this can happen in Chapter 15, on publicity and celebrations.

## BRICKS AND MORTAR

All of the great private educational institutions, and many of the public ones as well, have the names of generous donors gracing the lintels of classrooms, auditoriums, libraries, and other buildings and classrooms. Similarly, many of the best well-known arts venues are named for equally generous citizens or businesses: for example, Detroit's Ford Auditorium, former home of the Detroit Symphony Orchestra; and the Carlson School of Management at the University of Minnesota (named for Curt Carlson, founder of the Carlson Companies).

Each morning as I take my constitutional around the nature reserve across the street from my home, I see this kind of corporate philanthropy in microcosm. The mini-amphitheater overlooking the property bears a plaque acknowledging the contribution of our community bank in building it. Another commercial development company, which is often at odds with the community, is honored with a plaque on the floating bridge over the marshland, with a remark about its symbolic value in "building bridges between the company and the community."

It's clear that the development company "gets" the value of bricks-and-mortar giving. It needed some good public relations and high positive visibility to offset the negative reactions that its high-rise condominium projects often triggered among local residents. The condos had been blamed for increased traffic and pedestrian accidents in the area. The high-rises were also criticized for marring the pristine view from the south end of the nature preserve. The old bridge had rotted away after 20 years of exposure to harsh Minnesota winters. Without that simple wooden bridge, used by nearly every community resident several times a year, access to the south end of the preserve would have been nearly impossible. While residents may have been angry about the ruined vista, they still were grateful for the ability to traverse the marsh.

This is not to say that there still aren't protesters at City Council meetings when the developer submits yet another high-rise proposal for approval. However, the developer *can* point to the "extracurricular" benefits the community has gained as a result of the company's success in previous developments. There are few protesters who can beg ignorance of those benefits.

There are some minor problems with giving for bricks and mortar. Although buildings and other structures are fairly permanent, they are not immortal. I remember the case of the Palmer Classroom Building at the University of Minnesota. The building was less than 25 years old when the administration decided to demolish it (for several valid reasons). The new building on the site is significantly larger and is used for a purpose totally unrelated to the field that distinguished the eponymous Dr. Palmer.

After difficult discussions with the Palmer family, it was decided to name a wing of the new building "The Palmer Education Center"—in no way as great an honor or as visible as the original building. The university made great efforts to have the Palmer family engaged in activities that took place in the new Palmer Education Center. They had not been involved in activities in the old Palmer Classroom Building, but they truly appreciated the attention the new education center brought them, and eventually gave more money for teaching activities. It was a win–win situation, but not without initial difficulties, as the story here revealed.

In times of rapid corporate mergers and acquisitions, naming opportunities can become insignificant or troublesome for the charity. Take the example of the Target Corporation: It started as two parent companies, the Dayton Corporation of Minneapolis and the J.L. Hudson Company of Detroit. When the companies merged, the new entity became the Dayton-Hudson Corporation. About the time that the corporation's Target division became dominant, it purchased the venerable Marshall Field's. Now, all the department stores are known as Marshall Field's and the corporation and foundation have changed their names to Target. That's a lot of sand-blasting on the stone over the main entrance of a community library!

## Volunteering

### Executive Level

Demonstrating that your company supports volunteer efforts should start with the CEO. The CEO may enjoy running in charity marathons or mixing with other employees to build a playground. Many CEOs, however, find themselves on the boards of nonprofit organizations, where their managerial skills are greatly appreciated.

Most executives serve on these boards selflessly and with dedication to improving the community. But it is no secret in the business world that serving on nonprofit boards can be good for growing a business. Serving on boards is the ultimate networking experience. Where else can you mix with other business leaders in a totally noncompetitive atmosphere? Certainly not on the golf course!

The recently retired CEO of Wells Fargo, James Campbell, is a prime example of how board membership can be a win–win situation for all parts of the philanthropic equation. Before he retired, Campbell served on the boards of a large community foundation, the United Way, and the foundation of a large state university. Campbell's colleagues on the boards of these organizations represented the upper echelon of the local business community: law firms, industrial and commercial giants, political insiders, and public opinion leaders from the media. Each board meeting was another opportunity for these business leaders to interact on a personal level. They could see the ways in which their businesses could develop synergies while advancing the charitable causes that brought them together in the first place.

Although the lists of board members of these charities read much like a *Who's Who* in big business, by no means are they strictly old-boys' clubs. One person who shared the table with Campbell on one of those boards was the owner of a new website development company, who had barely been out of college for a decade. This up-and-coming website development company had a sterling list of clients, including one of the country's largest private foundations. Did the young entrepreneur get that account through a referral from Campbell? I can't answer that question, but it's a good possibility.

Some of the faces Campbell saw at any given board meeting were faces he was likely to see at others as well. Once a business leader has served successfully on one board, he or she will likely be asked to sit on others, and thus become even more collegial with potential customers or business partners.

How do you get on one of these influential boards? The best way is to sit on *any* board, just for starters. There is significant crossover between small organizations' boards and those in the big time. Executives whose businesses have grown and put them in a more prestigious and influential stratum of the community don't often abandon the nonprofit groups with which they've developed good relationships.

There may be a service in your state or community that acts as a matchmaker for company executives who want to serve on boards of local charities. The choice of organizations is varied, the chances for service are vast, and the opportunities to expand your business contacts are wide open. Contact your state office of volunteer services or the United Way for your community for a connection.

## Employee Volunteerism

In his 2002 State of the Union Address, President George W. Bush proposed the Freedom Corps. He called on all Americans to devote 4,000 hours over their lifetime to volunteering. He sees these acts of human kindness as one way to improve homeland security. Indeed, it may well be one method to achieve that goal. Most business leaders will not argue with Mr. Bush about the impact of volunteering on homeland security, but they also know that volunteering has effects that go far beyond security issues.

Giving employees time off to do volunteering is costly (see Exhibit 9.2). If time is money, how can they afford it? They make it part of the business plan from the start and budget for it.

Indianapolis-based Guidant, Inc., encourages its employees to volunteer with organizations of each employee's choice. The company assigns a dollar value to each hour volunteered and matches the hours with cash donations to the respective nonprofits. This shows Guidant's respect for its employees as individuals and spreads their giving power to a wide range of needs in the community.

Datalink, Inc., a Minnesota company with operations across the country, allows up to 16 hours per year of paid release time to employees for volunteer activities. This release time is contingent upon the volunteer activity relating to the citizenship program priorities of the company, particularly technology education and some areas of health. Even so, the options open in these fields are wide and can be loosely interpreted.

Law firms regularly perform services *pro bono* for nonprofit groups and indigent persons. Each partner makes his or her own decision regarding which cases to take, but the choices often must be approved by the other partners or a committee.

Even workaholics can find ways to become involved in volunteerism. How many of us have been confronted with the problem of unused sick leave, vacation, or overtime compensation hours? Too often, if we don't use it, we lose it. Creative managers have found ways to turn these hours into cash donated to various charities. Another option is to state that hours won't be "lost" if used by the employee for volunteering on company time. The hours might even be pooled and contributed for other employees to use for volunteering on company time.

---

**EXHIBIT 9.2**    VOLUNTEER TIME

Businesses support their employees in three ways by giving them paid time off to volunteer: You show that you care about their personal lives, that you care about their communities, and that you recognize the difference between vacation and community service.

*Source:* Reprinted with Special Permission of King Features Syndicate.

Smart business owners know that employee volunteerism has additional benefits. Those benefits reflect back on the company and often on the bottom line. When volunteers are out in the community, be it an individual coaching a Little League team, or a group that goes out to Race for the Cure, when the employees are spotted sporting the company's logo on a tee-shirt or uniform, it sends a strong message of community commitment to all who see it. Mentoring a parentless teen can open that young person's eyes to whole new career possibilities—even one with your company! When employees from different operational units and management strata volunteer together, it can improve internal communication, employee morale, and retention.

## The Cookie Dilemma:  On-Premises Fundraising

It happens every year in February or March: the Girl Scout cookie campaign. For your business, it may be in the fall shortly after school starts: the giant bars of chocolate appear (with or without almonds) on sale to benefit the elementary school library fund. At times, the competition for your employees' dollars for the (often fattening) products of these worthy charities can be fierce, especially when there are two or three parent-employees with children in the same school or troop. The dilemma over whom to buy from can be stressful for the individual employee who doesn't want to favor one coworker over another who is offering the same or similar products. "Why didn't she buy from me?" is *not* the kind of question you need to hear when trying to create a cooperative workplace.

Event sponsorship falls within this same category. The Multiple Sclerosis Society sponsors long-distance bike-a-thons. The Susan G. Komen Foundation's Race for the Cure for Breast Cancer has become practically an American institution. In any of these cases, you and your employees are asked by a rider or racer to donate $X$ amount of money for each mile in the event. The biggest money raiser often receives some sort of nonmonetary prize, although the value of the reward may still be substantial (e.g., a trip or cruise).

If you plan to allow this kind of fundraising to be conducted on company property, you may want to set limits and guidelines, such as alternating charities on a yearly basis.

# New Giving:  Venture Philanthropy and Social Entrepreneurism

## Venture Philanthropy

In the 1990s, creative minds in New Economy businesses in Texas, California, Virginia, and other parts of the United States put their ideas and their money together to experiment with innovative ways of bringing about social change. The concept is called *venture philanthropy*. Although the ideal model for venture philanthropy assumed a fast-growth, high-technology-oriented market, the concept still has had substantial success and validity in the slower market of the 2000s.

Venture philanthropy is a movement among newer business owners that seeks to apply some of the techniques of venture capitalism to the nonprofit world. Some of these techniques are:

- *Taking risks with careful management.* In fact, the Peninsula Community Foundation/ Center for Venture Philanthropy (PCF) recommends that the venture philanthropist establish a relationship akin to that of a managing partner with the fledgling nonprofit organization. Depending on the charity and the sophistication of its other board members, they may be very grateful and even anxious for someone with this kind of interest and expertise.

- *Creating performance measures for long-term outcomes.*

- *Developing close relationships between the donor (venture philanthropist) and the nonprofit (investee) organization.* Relationships of this kind involve more than money and the attention of one executive from your company. Are your employees and the rest of your management team ready to buy into this kind of long-term, intensive relationship?

- *Commitment to long-term funding of initiatives.* This means multiyear grants of between three and six years, according to PCF's standards. Such a high level of commitment may preclude your company from supporting others if you go through a down market for your products and services during this relationship.

- *Commitment to major funding for initiatives and organizational infrastructure.* What most startup charities have is a mission: a program that they want to accomplish. What too often keeps them from accomplishing this goal is the reluctance of less sophisticated or less committed donors to pay the infamous "administration and fundraising costs." It's great to buy food for a homeless shelter, but what good is the food if it spoils because there is no money for the maintenance contract on the refrigerator or the shelter is closed down for lack of insurance?

- *Identification of exit strategy for the venture philanthropist.* As the venture capitalist continues making investments in unprofitable companies, he knows that the time he's been waiting for will eventually come: when the company has a product or service to sell and is making profits. Similarly, the venture philanthropist looks to the day when the charity is self-supporting. The venture philanthropist makes investments with an eye toward creating infrastructures like a strong donor base, government contracts, or a profit-making venture within the charity that will sustain it in the future.

Who are some of these venture philanthropists and what are they doing?

Mario Morino, a retired software executive in Reston, Virginia, founded the Morino Institute there. The Morino Institute describes itself as "both catalyst and facilitator to help individuals, institutions and communities understand opportunities and risks presented by the Internet. It supports and collaborates with other organizations to enhance their own effectiveness; it also incubates and launches new initiatives."[2] Recognizing that the information age is quickly making old-economy skills obsolete, and that technology in and of itself is not a solution for all of today's problems, the Morino Institute seeks ways to make networked interactive communications technology an enabling tool for social change.

Not surprisingly, many of the leaders of the venture philanthropy movement came from Silicon Valley. These New Economy CEOs joined forces and funds to form the Entrepreneurs' Foundation. As its mission statement declares, the Entrepreneurs' Foundation seeks to inject philanthropy into the corporate culture of Silicon Valley and to make the community stronger "by applying venture capital principles to scale-up successful non-profit organizations."[3]

Why do they feel that this is necessary? Do successful nonprofits really need to be scaled up? Professionals and active volunteers and donors to nonprofits have long known that the demands on their organizations, especially those in the health and social service areas, have grown rapidly, despite the unprecedented economic growth of the 1990s economy and generally-perceived prosperity of most Americans, even after the market downturn. A recent report by Community Wealth Ventures for the Morino Institute's Venture Philanthropy Partners confirms and explains the pressures on nonprofits. "Their work, which once supplemented government efforts, has now in many cases taken the place of government. In fact, they've become their community's principal service provider for many human needs. However, resources have not increased in proportion to their increased responsibility."[4]

Just as for-profit venture capitalists don't invest in companies with long histories of profitability, the Entrepreneurs' Foundation does not support major, established charities. That means that mainline arts and educational institutions should not bank on getting support from a venture philanthropy fund, regardless of how innovative the specific program might be.

In contrast, newer groups with a track record that want to try something new to improve or expand their existing program would be prime candidates for venture philanthropy. Such a group might be surprised to have a member of the venture philanthropy group express interest in becoming a part of its board as a condition of the grant. For the nonprofit, this is not business as usual; it may or may not be allowed, depending on its bylaws. However, this *is* business as usual for the venture philanthropist.

One of the most successful and ambitious venture philanthropy funds is the Austin (Texas) Entrepreneur's Fund (AEF). The founders were motivated by particular concepts that are hallmarks of the movement. They want outcomes that have impacts not just on the actions of the people they help, but on their *thinking* as well. As business leaders, they see market concepts as a driver for designing social products and services. Similarly, their orientation in business leads them to view venture philanthropy as an investment, which is more effective than charity. What distinguishes the New Economy founders of this fund from others with a narrower view is their motivating belief that wealth creation should be balanced with social responsibility, and their recognition that the sustainability of social change must be supported through both philanthropic and earned income.

The AEF serves as an umbrella foundation for individual company donor-advised venture philanthropy funds, much like a community foundation. It's a good example of how these funds operate.

Leaders of the AEF target entrepreneurs of new companies to become venture philanthropists, even before the companies are profitable. How can this be done? AEF tells the potential venture philanthropist to establish a donor-advised fund without using cash by donating equity (usually stock options) into its pool. The donor chooses recipients to receive grants in the future, following a post-liquidity event such as an initial public offering (IPO) or acquisition. At that point, 10 percent of the fund proceeds are transferred to AEF itself to support its administration of the individual-company grants.

AEF requires its venture philanthropy partners to complete simple legal documents, including a consent resolution from the company's board of directors and a donor-advised fund agreement with AEF. It requires that the company's board approve grant recommendations. AEF also wants its members to become engaged in planning a giving and volunteerism strategy, and not just depend on AEF to make all charitable decisions.

## Social Entrepreneurism

Another take on venture philanthropy is the developing area of social entrepreneurism. Social entrepreneurism has two faces: Businesses that engage in socially responsible business practices; and nonprofit organizations that operate profit-making enterprises to fund and further their exempt activities. Taken in the context of social entrepreneurship, the enterprise may be involved in New Economy activities, often with a technology orientation.

A leading resource for this approach is the Institute for Social Entrepreneurs. It offers information and sponsors conferences on subjects in the field. The nonprofit Northland Institute assists entrepreneurial nonprofits in their missions, as well as offering training and support for social entrepreneurs.

Venture philanthropy and social entrepreneurism are characterized by risk. If your company finds its profits too dear to be subjected to risk even when given charitably, you can still follow the path of responsible and strategic individual or business support to nonprofits.

## SOCIALLY RESPONSIBLE INVESTING

As individuals, owners of closely-held, private companies do not always completely separate their personal finances from their company finances. This is especially true when it comes to making charitable donations. It matters little to them if the donation is written on the company checkbook or on a personal money-market check. All company profits belong to the owner, hence all profits are disbursed by the owner.

Owners of privately held companies also do not hold 100 percent of their net worth in their companies. Smart owners are careful to have highly diversified investment portfolios. As part of their corporate citizenship activities, they may want to look into different vehicles for socially responsible investing.

Investors can do the research and put their money with individual companies or go with socially responsible mutual funds like Calvert or Pax World Funds. According to the Social Investment Forum, in 1999, more than $2.2 trillion was invested in such funds.[5] That represents one in every eight dollars under professional management in the United States.

James Larson, a financial planner with Northeast Securities in Wayzata, Minnesota, deals only in socially responsible funds (SRFs). He claims that many of these funds are highly competitive, performing at or even 1 or 2 percent above the general market average.

Financial planners who are less specialized might typically have about 15 percent of their clients investing in SRFs. There is a trend: the old hippies of the 1960s and 1970s have had years of earning and have inherited wealth from hard-working parents. The old flower-power generation hasn't forgotten those "peace and love" values; now that they finally have some money to invest, they want to "walk the walk, and not just talk the talk" with it. With a little research, the committed investor will find that there is an SRF for every political, religious, or ethical concern, liberal or conservative; more than 250 SRFs are currently operating.

Aside from investing in these funds, shrewd investors will look at an SRF's prospectus and see which companies are represented in the portfolio. They can then make purchases of individual stocks, knowing that these companies have attained a high standard of corporate citizenship. What are some of the companies that are found most frequently in SRF portfolios? Examples include:

- Medtronic, in Pax World and Citizens Funds.
- Wells Fargo, in Parnassus and Pax World funds.
- General Mills, in Calvert and Pax World funds.
- Target and Best Buy, in Citizens Funds and others.

These outstanding companies go beyond the 1 percent charitable donation minimum of the Social Investment Forum to be approved as a socially responsible company for SRF investment.

What's the benefit for these good corporate citizens? Although there are dozens of advantages, here are just a few:

- Improved access to capital, particularly from socially conscious investors.
- Reduced operational risk, which can also lead to lower bank loan rates.

- Increased sales and customer loyalty.
- Enhanced brand image and reputation.

Another kind of socially responsible investing doesn't require you to send your money beyond the limits of your own community. Do some research into which banks in your area are lending to nonprofit organizations that fit your corporate citizenship criteria, and then do some banking with them. Taking $10,000 or even $100,000 of your liquid assets and putting it into a certificate of deposit is not taking much of a chance, but it indirectly supports the work of valuable nonprofits or loans to minority-owned businesses or affordable housing projects. It proves to the bank that doing good in the community will bring it other kinds of business.

It pays to be a good corporate citizen. It should pay business—both private and publicly owned—then, to invest some resources in developing a policy to include socially responsible investments. The payback will show in the bottom line.

## CAUSE-RELATED MARKETING

*Cause-related marketing* is a very broad catchphrase, and much of what it covers is integrated in other ways of giving. Cause-related marketing can be something very simple that makes a statement about what you and your company care about. Having a box at the cash register where customers can deposit coins that benefit a local charity is a kind of cause-related marketing. Sending a group of your employees out to participate in a walk-a-thon, while wearing the company logo on their caps or shirts, is another way to do it. How tough is it for you to enclose a donation envelope for a charity along with the billing information you send to your clients?

These simple methods have grown into more complicated and sophisticated schemes, and now are ubiquitous. It's nearly as difficult today to ignore cause-related marketing campaigns as it is to ignore most advertising.

### Paid Advertising

Cause-related marketing works. It's everywhere in the press. Looking at the Sunday, May 25, 2003, issue of the *Chicago Tribune,* readers saw numerous advertisements that had some connection to charitable activities:

- In connection with the exhibition of "Sue," the world's largest dinosaur fossil at the Field Museum, there were two ads. The first was a half-page advertisement in the front section, promoting the "Reading is Big" program at the *Chicago Tribune* Book Fair. You had to look closely at the ad to see the logo of the Target Corporation, but it was there.
- A full-page ad appeared on the back of the "Books" section that day, promoting the same event. This time, it was much clearer that Target was the sponsor for

"Reading is Big," and readers also learned that the major sponsor of the "Sue" exhibition was the McDonald's Corporation.

- Corporate sponsors of cultural events got double duty out of their donation dollars in the announcement of the schedule for the Chicago Symphony Orchestra's summer season at Ravinia, advertised in the "Entertainment" section. The sponsors' biggest opportunity for visibility was at Ravinia itself, but the schedule gave them additional exposure by announcing each company's sponsorship for its respective concert. The Chicago Symphony at Ravinia has both a regional and a national audience, and the sponsors reflect that fact. National sponsors catering to Ravinia's upscale audience included Merrill Lynch and Deloitte & Touche. The more local sponsors were Allegiance Telecom, Harris Private Bank, a radio station, and others.

- The arts fared well in the "Entertainment" section, as might be expected. Bud Light sponsored a blues concert series, and IBM, American Electric Power, and the Bravo Channel showed support for Cirque du Soleil.

- Moving on to the nationally syndicated *Parade* magazine, the national Ad Council teamed with the NAACP for an ad against teen drug use.

- Free advertising for business donors was most evident in the *Chicago Tribune Magazine*. Misericordia Siblings Association, an organization supporting people with mental and physical disabilities, bought page three to thank Chicago-based Northern Trust for its event underwriting. Its other sponsors were recognized as well: national corporations American Airlines and Young & Rubicam shared a line with local companies The LockUp Storage Centers and Practical Angle Framing & Gallery.

Cause-related marketing and cause branding are not new. Paul Newman's many food products, which have been on the market for years, state clearly on the label that the profits go to charity. Teenagers in today's world know Newman more for his food products than for his acting.

McDonald's supports a vast number of charities, but none is better known than the Ronald McDonald Houses. So successful has this campaign been for McDonald's that when the Target Corporation and Perkins' Restaurants tried to launch similar programs, they met with only limited success. In private conversations, the public would refer to such programs as "the Perkins Ronald McDonald House." Not a great way for a food chain like Perkins to try to distinguish itself from the competition.

Even if you are a widget manufacturer, it is likely that you will be advertising in publications outside of the widget industry, particularly publications that serve the widget market. Advertising space is generally an expensive proposition and you want to make the most of every inch. If you look at the preceding list of examples (particularly points two and three), you might be influenced to dedicate a portion of your widget advertisement to announcing that your company supports a charity related to the product or industry represented by that publication (e.g., the Aerospace Industry Hall of Fame Scholarship, or the Association for Safe Playgrounds Benevolent Fund). This does not mean that your scholarship donations have to be in the six figures. It should mean that your company is making a meaningful contribution to the cause, relative to your company's capacity to give and the needs of the nonprofit group.

Your company need not even make a contribution to an organization if you are buying advertising as part of a cause-related marketing strategy. Buying advertising space in the program of the local nonprofit orchestra or theater company will support the organization to a certain degree and get you higher visibility than the "free advertising" that is given to companies listed on the donor honor roll. This is particularly true for businesses in the hospitality industry. You want theater and music patrons to be able to locate your business for after-program meals, and lodgings for those who may have come from afar for a performance.

Many public radio and television stations publish program guides for their members. Your company could become an underwriter and thus get one or two on-air messages on a daily or weekly basis, in addition to having the company listed in the honor roll printed in the program guide. These messages still don't give consumers the information they need to contact you for a purchase. Buying advertising space in the program guide will solve this problem, give the station additional support, and reinforce the messages you are sending to the audience over the airways. Even if prospects are in the market for your product or service, they still must be exposed to your message more than seven times before there is sufficient name recognition for them to be receptive to your call. It takes even more exposure for them to initiate the transaction. Combining donations with advertising is an effective way of reinforcing the connection.

Members of the National Automobile Dealers Association (NADA) know that car dealers have a bad reputation in dealing with women. Across the country, numerous sexual harassment and discrimination suits have tarnished their reputation with women. Women are also leery of dealing with car dealers because they know that they are perceived as knowing less about cars than men, and therefore are more susceptible to being sold a lemon by a slick salesperson. Car dealers know from information produced by the NADA that women are involved in at least 85 percent of all car-buying decisions.[6] They know that they have to improve and clean up their image among women, and go even farther than that to gain some trust (see Exhibit 9.3).

An excellent example of this is found in a family of car dealerships that created a partnership with the Susan G. Komen Foundation and its well-known Race for the Cure. Luther dealerships could just have made a donation or allowed their names to be displayed along with other sponsors. But they wanted to make the connection between the not-so-obvious cause of breast cancer research and cars. The paid advertisement that Luther dealerships placed in local newspapers made the point through clever plays on words and images.

**EXHIBIT 9.3**    OVERT AND COVERT MESSAGES

The Luther Auto Dealers sent a doubly positive message to women when they advertised their sponsorship of the Race for the Cure.

THE LUTHER FAMILY OF DEALERSHIPS

# we know what drives you

A chance to change things for the better. The desire to contribute to the cause. An opportunity to set a good example. Whatever your reasons for participating in this year's Race For The Cure, the Luther Family of Dealerships understands. They're the same principles we've followed for more than 50 years.

**That's why we're proud to be a sponsor of the 2003 Twin Cities Race For The Cure.**

Run into any of our 23 local Luther dealerships today. You'll be delighted by how much we have to offer—and just how much we have in common.

**Register for the Race For The Cure at any Luther Family Dealership.**

Bloomington Acura Subaru
Brookdale Buick Pontiac GMC
Brookdale Honda
Brookdale Mitsubishi
Burnsville Volkswagen
Downtown Jaguar Daewoo Lotus
Rudy Luther's Hopkins Honda
Hopkins Town & Country Dodge
Hudson Chrysler Dodge Jeep
Infiniti of Bloomington
John Hirsch's Cambridge Motors
Luther Brookdale Chrysler Jeep
Luther Brookdale Mazda
Luther Lincoln Mercury
Luther Nissan Kia
Luther Westside Volkswagen
Metro Mitsubishi Hyundai
North Country Ford
Park Place Motorcars
Randy Iten Chevrolet Winnebago
Rudy Luther's Toyota
Toyota City
White Bear Acura Subaru Isuzu

Learn more about the Susan G. Komen Race For The Cure at www.racecure.org. Test drive over 12,000 Luther vehicles at www.lutherauto.com.

© 2003 Cuneo & Associates

**Luther** Automobile Dealerships

Proud Sponsor Of The Twin Cities Race For The Cure

*Source:* Luther Auto Dealers.

## "Free" Advertising

Becoming a treasured donor to a charity can have benefits unforeseen at the time of the contribution. One of these can be what is equivalent to free advertising, sometimes to a broad audience.

Virtually every nonprofit has a donor newsletter of some sort. By law, each must issue an annual report. These documents vary greatly in their sophistication and distribution. Some go strictly to a small donor base. Others are sent in massive direct-mail campaigns designed both to educate current and prospective donors and to motivate them to contribute.

Some newsletters are little more than lists of donors with a cover story on one of the charity's projects. Others have pages dedicated not just to listing donors, but to disseminating stories about their donors—including the businesses that support them in varied ways in their different programs. This is *free advertising*.

Larger charities have dedicated budgets for ads in the press and electronic media, and particularly in the press dedicated to business. It is not uncommon to see ads, either paid or donated as a public service by the media, that are basically a public thank-you to generous or creative business donors. They often tell little about the charity itself, but they tell a *lot* about the company featured. The big message is: "This is a company that our community should appreciate and respect." To other business owners, they say, "We could be telling this story about *your* company, too, if only you'd contribute."

Though generally not as highly compensated as the staff of a business marketing department, charities often have public relations staff persons who work hard to generate news in all media about the organization. They have contacts with editors, reporters, and publishers to produce stories that don't appear in the business pages, but are read and listened to by your customers. They, too, are always looking for a new angle to get their organization's name before the public. Your marketing staff or agency can work with the public relations volunteer or staff at the charity to create a press release or story with real public interest and quality (which, of course, highlights your company's role in the charity's program). The chances of that story making it to press or on the air are that much greater because of your staff's expertise.

Around Mother's Day every year, I see a spate of advertising with a common symbol: the pink ribbon that is the icon for the fight against breast cancer. The ads are all from department stores, offering to make a donation to a local anti-cancer group for research into the disease for each brassiere that is fitted to a customer. It's a great cause and a great connection, but there is no charitable advantage to shopping at one particular store, because everyone's doing it. *Timing* is important in charitable promotions.

Target Corporation donates a percentage of designated sales to specific schools when a customer fills out a registration form for the program. It's been a successful program. Office Max wanted to broaden its image beyond the business community and had its eye on a piece of the school supplies market. It now offers a similar program when a customer buys school supplies and shows a school registration card. Though there is some crossover in the target market, it probably does bring additional sales.

## Logistics

Conducting promotions with charities can be costly when the promotion involves coupons or labels. There are clearinghouses that can handle this part of the operation, and you and your financial staff can determine the cost-benefit ratio for any given promotion before you get started.

Another way of handling a contribution to charity, without having to count each label or coupon, is to strike an initial agreement with the charity. This could involve an upfront donation, and then provide for additional donations for each increment of $x$ units. In this way, the charity is assured that it will receive some benefit from the campaign, even if it is unsuccessful through no fault of its own. It will still be motivated to promote the campaign to the best of its abilities.

Your cause-related marketing campaign need not be a year-round effort, nor do you have to commit to one charity *ad infinitum*. Your corporate contributions plan may call for you to concentrate on only one charity per year, and then move on to another group or cause.

You may choose to partner with a charity for a specific occasion. An effective short-term partnership might be when a restaurant opens in a new location. You can include a coupon as part of your promotional flyer, your newspaper ads, or even your website. For each coupon redeemed during the opening event, day, or week, you will make a donation to your charity partner. Besides attracting hungry patrons in general, you will motivate donors, volunteers, and friends of your charitable partner. The same can be done if you sell window shades.

The positive side of changing charities is that you are able to reach the market associated with each of them. The negative side is that the exposure time may not be sufficient for you to create an impression or relationship. Getting the customer in the door for the first sale is what you want, to help you create a relationship that will keep them coming back even when the charitable partnership has terminated.

## Cause-Related Marketing versus Sponsorship

It seems that every charity has either a marathon or golf tournament these days. If your company is asked to sponsor a mile or kilometer for the marathon, $x$ number of your employees can be registered for free and your company's name will appear on the tee-shirt for finishers, as well as in the program and on a banner. At the golf tournament, you receive similar courtesies for your employees, and you get the extra benefit of being able to hand out samples of your product at "your" hole. It's great visibility.

Sponsoring events, such as the Mother's Day celebration at the Minnesota Zoo, gives a small florist that specializes in nontraditional designs entrée to an audience that enjoys the jungle atmosphere of the zoo's indoor habitat (see Exhibit 9.4). It also gives them free exposure in the ad the zoo bought to promote the event. Yes, the advertisement is paid partially through the florist's sponsorship donation, but it still costs less than buying an ad for its own purposes: the zoo gets the nonprofit advertising rate *and* the florist gets the bonus of being associated with a popular cause.

**EXHIBIT 9.4    TARGETING NEW AUDIENCES**

Sponsoring the Mother's Day brunch at the Minnesota Zoo was a different way for Stems and Vines to reach an audience that would appreciate its untraditional floral designs.

## Celebrate Mother's Day
### in a TROPICAL Way—
#### Come for Brunch at the Minnesota Zoo!
Treat your mom to a special Mother's Day Brunch. Our Tropics Trail is the perfect backdrop for this special occasion. Pre-registration is necessary for the brunch.

Sponsored by:

STEMS *and* VINES
FLOWERS BY DESIGN

**Sunday, May 11, 2003**
**8:30 am–2:30 pm • Tropics Atrium**
**For reservations, call 952.953.0667**

MINNESOTA ZOO

*Source:* Minnesota Zoo. © Shannon Ruschmeyer for Minnesota Zoo.

## Cautionary Notes

Don't underestimate the intelligence of your target market. They quickly and easily recognize two major mistakes that businesses make in cause-related marketing.

*Hopping on the Bandwagon.*    The case of the pink ribbon is typical of bandwagoning. The target market for brassieres is exclusively women. The vast majority of people who develop breast cancer are women. It seems to be an obvious connection, and it *is* a good one. But if your objective is to stand out from the crowd, this charity may not be your best choice, especially if all your competitors are doing this same promotion. Women can see that you may not be doing it out of any real commitment to women and the cause, but because everyone else is doing it. Adopting a day-care center or battered women's shelter might demonstrate both support and thoughtfulness.

Women care about breast cancer, but it's not the only thing they care about that affects females. The Women's Funding Network reported in 2003 that, despite the dismal condition of the economy in 2002, giving to women's funds and foundations grew at an unprecedented rate.[7] These data referred to philanthropic institutions that primarily fund grassroots organizations supporting women and girls. These are not organizations that address breast cancer, however important that cause may be.

Two things can be learned from this report: Women have a lot of money to give, and women care about many things other than breast cancer. If your company wants to distinguish itself from the pack, look at other charities that help women and develop a relationship and a program to work together.

*Self-Aggrandizement.*    This means tooting your own horn too loudly and thereby undermining the credibility of your philanthropic intent. Exemplifying this is the electrical utility company that bought a full-page ad in its local business magazine to highlight its support of a peregrine falcon reintroduction program. The program runs on an extremely small budget. The utility's main contribution was allowing researchers to provide nest boxes for these natural cliff-dwellers on the company's smokestacks.

The fact of the matter is that the advertisement demonstrating the utility's commitment to the environment (in the form of support for falcons) cost far more than the actual value of the company's annual support for the bird program. This is not to say that the ad was ineffective in creating a positive image of a polluting industry. The uninformed general public was easily fooled. Environmentalists were not, and they continue to plague the company by protesting storage practices at its nuclear power plants.

## GIVING OPTIONS CHECKLIST

❐    Federated charities and community funds

❐    Matching gifts

❐    Challenge grants

- ❑  Lead gifts
- ❑  Over-the-top gifts
- ❑  Tributes and awards
- ❑  In-kind gifts of products and services
- ❑  Hiring of the handicapped
- ❑  Purchase of products and services from nonprofits
- ❑  Scholarships
- ❑  Bricks and mortar
- ❑  Volunteering
- ❑  Venture philanthropy
- ❑  Social entrepreneurism
- ❑  Socially responsible investing
- ❑  Cause-related marketing

# Relating Corporate Citizenship Activities to the Company's Products, Services, and Mission

Only you and your employees know what your products and services are and how they relate to your mission. The key to a successful corporate citizenship program is finding the logical match between the kinds of organizations you will support (including the activities you will conduct to support them) and what your company is in business to do to make a profit. Without that kind of match, you might as well be playing "charity roulette."

It would be impossible in this book to address every business product or service. What we can do is look at many of the kinds of causes that exist and give some examples of how and where they fit with business. It would be impossible for me to list and discuss every cause and its implications for business, especially as every community is unique. However, many common causes are covered in the following material, and others are listed in the checklist at the end of the chapter.

Owners of closely held businesses often think that because the company's profits are legally theirs, it follows that their charitable interests are also the best ones for the company. This is a serious fallacy.

Just because the owner of a drapery manufacturing company is an avid fly-fisher, it is not likely that most employees on the sewing floor will share that passion; they might find it hard to whip up enthusiasm for support of Trout Unlimited. Neither are the majority of the company's clients going to identify with this worthy environmental organization.

Finding the right cause or causes is one of the most difficult parts of creating your company's plan. If you have but one product or service, making the connection is easier.

For the publisher of children's educational books, it is a no-brainer: support of literacy at the K-12 level.

A twist on this might be support of adult literacy programs. Research shows that children whose parents read to them have higher reading achievement than those who don't. If parents are illiterate, it's clear that they will not read to their children, and the trickle-down effect is self-evident. In communities with high immigrant populations, this might also translate into support of programs for English as a Second Language for adults.

## Contemplating Cause Options

When laying out your plan, it is best *not* to name specific organizations unless it is one such as United Way. Preselected charities such as these should have either a particularly wide and popular base, or a long-established and positive relationship with your company. The idea of the plan is to allow for focus in giving areas, while recognizing that charities come and go or gain and lose strength over time.

## Quality-of-Life Programs

There are a couple ways of looking at charities and charitable activities. There are those that fall under "quality of life" (a general enhancement of the competitive context) and that generally do not have *direct* benefit back to business.

### Arts and Culture

Projects in the arts and support of cultural institutions are often viewed as the bailiwick of big business. Advertisements for major art exhibitions usually exhibit the names and logos of high-profile corporations as sponsors. However, as discussed in Chapter 3, culture and the arts are catalysts for revenue for dozens of collateral businesses that compose a healthy local economy.

Arts need not be viewed exclusively as the domain of the wealthy or highly educated elite. Many communities support free open-air summer concerts with music that ranges from the police band to teenager's rock groups. The audiences for these programs are truly democratic. Such programs, again, add to the quality of life for the entire community—including your lower-wage assembly and sales employees and their families.

### K–12 Education and Children

It is the rare school, public or private, that does not engage in fundraising at least once or twice a year. In the past, the fundraising activities were aimed at extracurricular programs such as sports, cheerleading, or the band. Today, private fundraising is often used to purchase technology—or indeed, any capital expenditure beyond the physical structure that houses the school. It is not inconceivable that in the near future we will be seeing company names adorning school football fields or on student transportation buses, as schools attempt all possible means of gaining support for essential services.

School fundraising has gone far beyond the familiar bake sale or car wash. Much of it is now out of the hands of students, teachers, and administrators, or even the PTA. Concerned citizens outside of the scholastic domain are forming private foundations, the sole purpose of which is to raise funds for a particular school or school district, and to keep control of the money out of the hands of desperate school board members and administrators. Institutions of higher education have long used this tactic to ensure that funds raised, for example, for an endowed professorship will be used only for that purpose, and will not be redirected to cover other expenses, such as legal costs.

K-12 educational programs are categorized as a quality-of-life option here because of the extreme long-term nature of the return on investment. Most business owners are looking for well-educated and competently trained employees. They also need a market that can afford their products and services; this requires a similar population of adequately paid persons. We expect our schools to produce a body of employees and consumers to fit both of these bills. Waiting 12 years for the pupil who benefits from your company's donation or volunteer program to graduate, and then either buy your product or join your firm, is an exercise in both patience and faith.

It is an adage that a community is only as good as its schools. Whether your company serves a local or global market, you and many of your employees live in a fairly defined geographic community. It only makes sense to invest in the schools—yes, through your taxes, but also philanthropically—to maintain the quality of that community.

Beyond the walls of the school, the number and kinds of organizations that benefit children are countless. We all were children at one time, and most of us are either parents or aunts and uncles. As individuals, we all have a stake in children.

The large national organizations, such as Boy and Girl Scouts, have regional councils and local troops. On the local level, they seldom seek major grants from business. The question, as with school fundraising, is whether your company will permit them to sell their famous cookies, or calendars, or Christmas trees, or whatever on your company's premises. How will you make that decision? Will you leave it up to the employee committee charged with corporate citizenship activities, or exempt these activities from the policy?

Virtually every community has youth organizations that are unique to its locale. They do not get support, either financially or programmatically, from a parent organization; consequently, they are highly responsive to the needs of their particular clientele.

When developing your corporate citizenship plan, weigh the pros and cons of these two different approaches to addressing the needs of youth, and the administration, credibility, stability, and visibility of each organization. This thoughtful deliberation will serve you well in every category of programming where you have the options of supporting an independent group or the local affiliate of a national charity.

## Housing/Homelessness

You intend to pay your employees a fair wage. In years past, the rule of thumb was that one-quarter of a worker's wages was the acceptable percentage to be used for housing. That ratio changed in the 1980s, so that now fully one-third of our salaries goes toward housing.

There has been a nationwide shortage of housing at all levels for nearly a decade in most larger urban areas of the country. The biggest shortfall is in the category called "affordable." The definition of *affordable* varies, but generally it is fixed at a figure of $X$ times the poverty level of a particular community, or at $Y$ percentage of the area's median income.

Unfortunately, the term *affordable* has gained an undeservedly bad connotation through its connection to failed public housing projects, so many upper-income community residents often come out to fight such developments in their midst. What they fail to see is that persons who provide essential services, such as teachers, police officers, firefighters, other civil servants, and nonprofit managers, very often are those who qualify for affordable housing. Without such accommodations nearby, the community finds it hard to recruit these valuable workers and the communal quality of life (remember *competitive context?*) suffers—not to mention its safety. In reality, affordable housing is better characterized as *workforce* housing. Hence, the line between quality of life and enlightened self-interest for employers.

Construction, contracting, and development firms have claimed that they lose money on lower-priced units. They are not exaggerating these claims. The economic impact of workforce housing is underscored by the results of a study on the subject done in the metropolitan Twin Cities area. The report brought out these points:

- Private developers may lose about $31,000 per unit for owner units, and $43,000 per rental unit.

- But, for each dollar invested in workforce housing, $8.13 is generated in economic benefits for the community at large. This harkens back to the economic ripple effect demonstrated for investments in the arts (discussed earlier).[1]

Recognizing the real losses and subsequent disincentives for private business to create affordable housing, the nonprofit sector has stepped up to the plate. Probably the best-known nonprofit builder is Habitat for Humanity. Its approach combines private donations, volunteer labor, and sweat equity to build single-unit homes for families. Building a Habitat for Humanity house has become a popular group volunteer activity for many companies, which find that it also builds esprit de corps across job titles in big business.

Making an investment in affordable housing need not even be done through non-profit avenues. Using the market for social advancement should not be outside the scope of any company's corporate citizenship plan, as demonstrated in Chapter 9. A small amount of research should reveal which banks in your community are involved in financing affordable housing projects. Buying a certificate of deposit with such a financial institution can bring good housing for low-wage earners to the community and a favorable return on investment to your company.

Homeless persons are not always the dregs of society that is the stereotype. The fact is that a good percentage of persons who use facilities for the homeless, such as shelters and soup kitchens, have full-time jobs—and this is not a recent development.

Organizations that address the needs of homeless persons need money, but your company can also use different resources to help this cause. Volunteering and donations of food through employee drives are just two ways to help. If your company is involved in growing, processing, packaging, or distributing food at any level, associating with Second Harvest or a local food bank makes good business sense on a strategic level, beyond its value as an improvement to the community's quality of life.

## Social Services

*Social services* is a catch-all descriptor for a huge sector of organizations offering a vast spectrum of benefits to all parts of your community. Many of them are run by sectarian groups that offer services to those in need regardless of their faith. Hence, be sure, when you write your criteria for consideration, that you do not categorically rule them out if you exclude religious groups from your giving program.

Many of your community's social service agencies will be beneficiaries of your local United Way campaign. It's a good thing that the United Way is the biggest supporter of social services. Unlike the arts or higher education, which often have well-heeled constituencies, social services agencies generally do not have clients who can donate back once their immediate needs have been met.

Social service agencies are the most susceptible to economic hard times. The *Giving USA* report for 2002, published by the American Association of Fundraising Counsel Trust for Philanthropy, showed human services as taking the biggest hit in an overall down year for charities: donations fell 11.4 percent (after inflation) from the previous year.[2] Some of this relates directly to their dependence on workplace giving programs such as United Way, since layoffs were all too common in participating companies. Yet, these are the agencies that your company's laid-off workers turn to for help with mental health counseling, job retraining, debt counseling and management, and so on during unemployment.

Giving to the United Way at the corporate level addresses the quality of life on a broad scale. Targeting grants to one or two nonprofit programs that provide for the needs of your employees (or former employees) may help advance some of your short-term strategic business goals.

## Federated Charities

The largest national nonsectarian federated charity is the United Way. The United Way is an umbrella organization for a vast array of national and local organizations, most of which are social services groups. Each community that hosts a United Way determines which local organizations will qualify for its funding and technical assistance.

The United Way raises the majority of its funds through workplace giving. Businesses make arrangements through their payroll offices to have voluntary donations from employees deducted regularly or periodically from paychecks. The United Way has staff to help companies conduct programs and events to stimulate giving. It's a system that is easily implemented and maintained and has been successful for years.

At one time, the United Way held exclusive rights to workplace giving in private business. The Combined Federal Campaign, offered to government employees, gave them the opportunity to give not only to U.S.-based charities, but to international groups as well. For more than a decade now, companies have been able to offer their employees a variety of workplace giving options beyond United Way.

In many communities, additional federated charities have been formed through alliances of similar organizations to facilitate workplace giving for the arts and culture, health groups, environmental, or even grassroots charities. Sectarian organizations have federated charities as well, and these may suit your company if it is oriented toward a religious market.

## Social Justice/Legal Aid

Supporting these causes is a natural for law firms and legal services companies. Law firms often give cash, but one of the more common ways of giving is by doing *pro bono* work at the request of a legal aid organization. Other firms offer free or reduced-fee services, particularly in the hospitality industry, for immigrants. Look carefully around the hotel the next time you are at an industry convention in a major city, and you will see the rainbow of complexions that is the face of the new America. Whether they are here legally or not, these persons are holding jobs that are the first step on the road to the American dream, and they are unquestionably an important part of our economy. When they need help, either for themselves or to bring a relative to the United States, they are likely to use nonprofit legal services.

## International

When discussing quality of life, we cannot ignore the fact that people who live far beyond the borders of our own cities and states have growing influence on our local communities. More and more, people are coming to agree that people on Earth indeed live in a global village. The whole world is engaged in an interdependent global economy. Though several big commodities—notably oil, food, and labor—gain the majority of attention in the media, one of the United States' biggest trade commodities is entertainment. Our movies, television programs, and music are among the largest producers of revenue in the world marketplace. It is the rare business these days that is not touched either by foreign trade or foreign competition.

We are bigger importers than we realize or care to admit. Where are your company's components coming from? What countries are suppliers? Look deep into the supply chain. Much of the petroleum and oil that fuel the business of our country comes not only from the Middle East, but also from poor countries in Asia and Latin America. Although American shoppers may look for the union label when buying apparel, it is apparent that a huge percentage of our clothing and home products are produced in Third World countries where labor is cheap. For years, America's trade balance has been tilted in favor of our foreign trading partners. If your company doesn't export, the chances are that many of your customers do. If their businesses fail, it endangers your business.

The image of international charities often is based on the face of a hungry child living in squalor in a Third World country. This tactic is effective in motivating hundreds of thousands of unsophisticated donors to make the small donations that are the lifeblood of these charities, but it fails to communicate the other highly important work that most of them do in building stronger economic infrastructures in the places where they operate. Organizations like CARE, Oxfam, Church World Service, and others all have extensive, successful programs that address your company's business interests at some point in the chain of supply and demand: agriculture, credit cooperatives and micro-lending, building schools and clinics, sanitation, and so on. All these efforts are designed to uplift the foreign country's quality of life, making the people better producers of your imported products or consumers of your exports.

If your company has operations in a foreign country, you may wish to make charitable contributions in local currency but find that there is a vacuum of trustworthy, credible indigenous nonprofits to work with. Also, the tax laws of your host country may not make it favorable for you to support local nonprofit groups. The country office of most U.S.-based charities generally will be able to accept your local-currency donation and still make it possible for you to take a deduction on your U.S. taxes.

## Environment

The absolute most basic element of quality of life is the environment. The media coverage of industrial disasters (such as the Union Carbide air-pollution holocaust in Bhopal, India, and the Exxon *Valdez* oil spill in Alaska) brought worldwide attention to environmental accidents with limited geographic scope, but extensive damage to both the environment and the humans and wildlife that inhabit it. If your company produces pollution that goes anywhere beyond the walls of your plant, it is a smart idea for you to support environmental causes for one big reason: preemptive reparations, or what I like to call "reputation insurance."

The Ford Motor Company produces products that are recognized as being major contributors to air pollution. For the past couple of years, Ford has been promoting its "Heroes for the Planet" awards program. The Ford award recognizes individuals and organizations that do outstanding work and research in environmental protection and restoration. Ford promotes the program in print advertising, but also gets double duty out of its sponsorship of environmental programs on public television stations by promoting the "Heroes" during its sponsorship announcements. Ford knows that the public knows it is a major polluter. By sponsoring the "Heroes" awards, Ford indirectly acknowledges this and shows its commitment to making amends.

Ford also makes effective use of its PBS environmental programming sponsorships when it shows the vast fields of tires it recycles annually. These ads tell the affluent audience of PBS viewers that it's okay to buy Ford products because it's doing its best to mitigate the environmental damage it creates.

Ford does its advertising on a national basis because it is a national—indeed, multinational—corporation. Your local public television or radio station also needs local underwriting for the same programs. You can hitch your company's wagonfull of effluents to Ford's star, as long as your company is truthfully doing its best to be a good environmental citizen.

One of the cheaper ways to make an environmental statement is the "Adopt a Highway" program, popular in most states and sponsored by the Department of Transportation or Highways. For a small fee, your company's name is shown on highway signs announcing that it will be cleaning trash from the roadside during the year. It's a great opportunity for your company to get publicity with the vast number of travelers along that route. It's also a good opportunity for you to create an event for employees that includes a picnic, beach or pool party, or other treat following the cleanup.

Such has been the popularity of these adoption programs that some states are running out of adoptable highway miles. Alternative cleanup sites are now offered for parks or riverbanks. Cleanup activities afford excellent opportunities for publicity, so be sure to have a photographer along to chronicle the event and encourage all participants to wear company regalia.

## STRATEGIC PROGRAMS

In many ways, all philanthropic activities relate to a community's quality of life. After all, *philanthropy* in its strictest translation means "love of one's fellow." The line between quality-of-life giving and a gift that is a strategic investment for your company can be thin or blurred. If this were not so, and there were a guaranteed payback for your business, it is likely that your donation would be disqualified for a tax deduction. However, some ways of giving that still qualify as charity can give you better odds of receiving more direct benefit.

### Higher Education Scholarships and Internships

There is nothing like a generous scholarship to raise awareness of your company among bright, talented young people who may want to work for their generous benefactor some day. How successful you are in your goal of recruiting your sponsored scholars onto the company payroll after graduation depends to some degree on how you structure that scholarship program.

Millions of scholarship dollars go unawarded every year, despite the existence of hundreds of qualified students who need financial aid. There are two primary reasons for this waste. First, the requirements or eligibility criteria are unreasonably and often unwisely narrow; second, the students are unaware that the scholarship exists.

Although it seems like a good idea to establish a minimum grade-point average for scholarships, this can backfire if you are seeking a student with particular interests. Consider this scenario:

> Your company is seeking an entry-level technician with a bachelor's degree in microbiology. You create a scholarship at the local state university for students in microbiology, setting an overall grade-point average of 3.0 for applicants to be considered.
>
> There is a student whose mother works in your company cafeteria who is studying microbiology, but money is scarce in the family and the student is putting in a lot of hours at the neighborhood fast-food restaurant to make tuition costs. She sure could use your scholarship. She has done well in her biology, microbiology, and other science courses, achieving a 3.6 grade-point average in those areas. Her overall average, however, is somewhat below 3.0, because she didn't do well in the foreign-language and philosophy classes required for graduation.
>
> Clearly, this promising microbiologist cannot be considered for your company's scholarship as written. Had you structured it more strategically and required an overall grade-point average of only 2.8, with a 3.2 average in biology courses, the result might be different—and your chances of hiring the grateful student after graduation would be greatly increased. Simply put, do not make scholarship requirements or restrictions too tight.

When students don't know that your scholarship exists, they cannot apply for it. That means that you have no opportunity to connect with and cultivate the student for future employment.

An institution of higher learning may hold an endowment your company has donated for a scholarship, or may have a document stating that your company will make annual gifts to support scholarships. This, however, does not always mean that the institution is going to go out of its way to promote and distribute the money. Staff shortages are endemic at most colleges and universities, and the financial aid office, which lacks a teaching mission, is a low priority in the institution's bureaucracy.

Simple advertising of your scholarship is a good way to get the word out. Print a poster for financial aid officers and student services staff to post in public areas on campus. Take out an ad in the student newspaper. You can use the same ad or poster year after year.

Develop a relationship with a faculty member in your area of interest. They all have student advisees whom they can steer in the direction of your company's scholarship.

Another highly valuable alternative to traditional scholarship awards is a paid internship. Paid internships help the students financially and give them a start on a professional resume. Your staff may have to exert some additional effort in dealing with interns, but these arrangements give you an excellent opportunity to evaluate whether you wish to offer the intern a job with the company after graduation.

## Research

It's no coincidence that Silicon Valley computer companies developed in the San Francisco Bay area. Stanford University is in Palo Alto. Nor it is surprising that the University of Michigan has long held supremacy in automotive engineering, with the headquarters of the "Big Three" automobile manufacturers nearby in the Detroit area. The University of Minnesota's chemical engineering department and industry leader 3M work in a symbiotic relationship. The key to all of these successful relationships is research.

Your company may have a research and development department. The knowledge and techniques developed there are directed specifically and exclusively for your company's benefit. The information is proprietary and often closely guarded. It also is expensive.

Donations toward faculty research at a university or technical college can be directed toward your specific interest without endangering the tax-deductible status of the gift. What you cannot control is the dissemination of the results. "Publish or perish" is an academic imperative that is taken very seriously by faculty seeking tenure and promotion. Therefore, depending on your competition, underwriting research at academic institutions may or may not be a good idea for your business. You must weigh the risk of your competition reading published results and acting on them against the benefits of relatively cheap research and development.

## SOCIAL INVESTING

Writing out a check to a charity is not the only way to achieve a good for society that will also accomplish a goal for your company or yourself. In this chapter, we've already discussed the idea of buying a certificate of deposit at a bank that invests in affordable housing in "redlined" areas.

There are more traditional ways to invest, such as playing the stock market and with mutual funds. Your board's finance committee must decide if it wants to set aside part of the company's (or, in the case of a privately held business, your family's) investment portfolio for corporations that meet high ethical standards in particular areas. There are mutual funds that invest in companies that deal with social problems: orphan-drugs companies, brownfields cleanups, and the like. The Big Three areas that are in the eye of the general public are:

1.  Environmental issues, from waste production and disposal, to pollution prevention, to efficiency in resource use.

2.  Workplace standards, including safety and ergonomics, training, compensation, work/family balance, and layoff policies.

3.  Community involvement that encompasses charitable donations, volunteerism, and so forth.

Investors can do the research and put their money with individual companies, or go with socially responsible mutual funds (SRFs) such as Calvert or Pax World Funds.

## Dealing with Disasters and Emergencies

Consider these scenarios: The river running through low-income neighborhoods of your town floods, leaving dozens of families—including many of your employees—homeless. Virtually no one has flood insurance. A fire breaks out in an apartment building and one of your employees dies in it, leaving a widow and three children. The lease holds the landlord blameless and your employee has no renter's insurance. These nonunionized hourly employees are not eligible for life insurance under your company's human resources policies and have none of their own. These are situations that truly fit the description of "charity cases."

Often, a local bank will set up a fund to receive contributions for the aid and relief of victims of such emergencies and disasters. The money will be put to a charitable use, but it does not qualify for a charitable tax deduction. You can make a donation to that bank fund, or directly to the family, that in the end will be a nondeductible expenditure, and that indeed is charity. Alternatively, you can find a nonprofit organization that deals with such emergencies—the Red Cross or Salvation Army, for example—that will administer your donation to the victims. Yes, some money will be taken out for administrative costs, but you will receive a tax deduction for the contribution. The choice is yours.

## Proactive Giving and Strategic Alliances

Once you have chosen your cause, you must find a way to distinguish your company. A pink ribbon symbolizes the fight against breast cancer. It appears frequently in ads for department stores, which offer a donation to the cause each time a customer gets fitted for a new brassiere. The connection between breast cancer and brassieres is an easy one to make and appeals to virtually all women. But when all stores in a market area offer the same program, why should any given woman shop at your store when she can get the same deal at the competition?

Finding something that is unique is the key to bringing in the charity-minded customer. Rather than give to a national breast-cancer organization, why not contact a local hospital and use your donations to underwrite prevention and treatment efforts there? With such a strategic alliance, the owner of the specialty lingerie shop in a suburban strip mall can then compete against the department stores for the same market.

## CHECKLIST OF CATEGORIES FOR GIVING

- ❏ Arts and culture
- ❏ K-12 education
- ❏ Sectarian causes
- ❏ Higher and vocational education
- ❏ Women's organizations
- ❏ Housing
- ❏ Social justice/legal aid
- ❏ Social services
- ❏ Federated charities
- ❏ Scholarships
- ❏ Sponsored research
- ❏ Health/diseases
- ❏ Ethnic institutions
- ❏ Libraries
- ❏ Adult literacy
- ❏ Senior citizens
- ❏ Socially responsible investing
- ❏ Veterans
- ❏ Emergency campaigns
- ❏ Environment
- ❏ International
- ❏ Civic celebrations
- ❏ Industry-related organizations
- ❏ Hunger
- ❏ Blood/marrow drives
- ❏ Adopt-a-highway

## CHAPTER 11

# Researching Possible Investments

Once your team has chosen a strategic direction for giving, you have two choices in deciding how your company will give: proactively or reactively. You have worked too hard earning profits to give away to become an "accidental philanthropist" and just give on a whim to whatever cause presents itself when you're in a generous mood. Deciding how you will give will have much to do with how you seek out organizations to support.

## NARROWING THE FIELD FOR STRATEGIC ALLIANCES AND PROACTIVE GIVING

Most people and institutions are reactive in their giving; that is, they don't give unless they are asked. It's a simple scenario: Someone asks you for a contribution. It may be a face-to-face solicitation, when your employee or a customer approaches you to give. In these cases, you are likely to give an answer (yes or no) on the spot, and that will be the end of the solicitation.

The chances that you will be called at the office by a telemarketer asking for donations are slim, but it is not out of the realm of possibility. Direct-mail solicitors also try to avoid sending requests to business addresses. There *are* numerous exceptions to these two latter situations, particularly for charities that are allied to your industry or commercial associations.

Whether or not you whip out your checkbook immediately, or call your Accounts Payable clerk to handle the matter, most likely you will continue to receive calls and letters asking for gifts. Direct-mail and telemarketing fundraisers count on asking prospective donors seven to eleven times in order to raise the first donation. After that, they expect to ask current donors an average of three times before the next check is mailed.

To avoid an overflowing bin for recycling the flood of requests, you have three options:

1. Contact the Direct Mail Marketing Association (*www.dmaconsumers.org/consumer assistance.html*) and follow the directions to be removed from mailing lists.

2.  Get your telephone number registered with your state's "do not call" list, as well as the federal list.

3.  Create and activate policies to support a proactive giving program.

In proactive giving, *you* take the initiative to seek out one or more charitable groups or causes with which to create exclusive or semi-exclusive strategic partnerships; you don't wait for them to ask for a contribution. Following this route requires a substantial amount of upfront research and relationship building, but will save you time and effort in the long run.

## STEPS TO PROACTIVE GIVING

### Review

When you start researching your potential partners, first review your company's philanthropic mission, the methods you have selected for your giving efforts, and other considerations such as the geographic impact area. Review also the donations you have made in the past several years, if any, to charities that meet the current criteria. Make special note of those who went the extra mile to thank you or to provide special reports, or who have other important ties to your company (customer relationship, volunteer connections, etc.).

This is the point where you will be matching your company's strategic philanthropic mission to that of available charitable partners. Exhibit 11.1 shows an outstanding example of an excellent strategic partnership between two parties that, on the surface, have little connection.

Courage Center is a nationally known physical rehabilitation center for persons with disabilities stemming from all kinds of causes: congenital defects, strokes, and other diseases. Others come to Courage Center because they have been severely injured in car accidents.

One very popular method of fundraising at Courage Center is the sale of donated cars, a practice that is gaining ground with many different kinds of nonprofits. Many of the cars donated can be resold with little or no work. Others need substantial mechanical or body work or need to be refitted as special-use vehicles for persons leaving Courage Center.

The connection for Abra, therefore, is logical on two levels. First, Abra recognizes that some of the cars it fixes for regular clients may have been involved in accidents that resulted in personal injuries requiring rehabilitation at Courage Center. Abra says, in effect, that it cares not only about the body of the damaged car, but also for the human body—the damaged *human being*—who drove or was injured by that car.

On the other level, Abra is doing what it does best: fixing cars. It makes sense to use Abra's existing expertise and resources instead of trying to do something that doesn't relate to its business (for example, serving meals at a homeless shelter). Where is the connection between auto body repair and homelessness (except that too many homeless persons live out of their cars)?

**EXHIBIT 11.1** STRATEGIC PARTNERSHIP

Donated cars are a significant source of income for Courage Center. Cars and trucks are the focus of business for Abra. Their common interest in cars brought the two together for a successful partnership.

# DONATE YOUR CAR OR BOAT TO COURAGE CENTER

- **AVOID THE HASSLE AND COST** of trading or selling your vehicle.
- **GET A TAX DEDUCTION** based on fair market value.
- Proceeds **SUPPORT COURAGE SERVICES** for people with disabilities to reach their full potential.

Cars for Courage

## SATURDAY, MAY 31, 9AM – 12PM

*DROP OFF YOUR VEHICLE\*, KEYS AND TITLE AT*
**COURAGE CENTER, 3915 GOLDEN VALLEY RD., GOLDEN VALLEY,**
**COURAGE ST. CROIX, 1460 CURVE CREST BLVD., STILLWATER,**
*OR ANY OF THESE ABRA LOCATIONS:*

**AUTO BODY & GLASS**

**Arden Hills** . . . . . . . . 3777 Lexington Ave. N.
**Burnsville** . . . . . . . . . 510 Southcross Drive
**Plymouth** . . . . . . . . . 11040 Hwy 55
**Eden Prairie** . . . . . . . 9020 Aztec Dr.

\* Vehicles must be 1989 or newer and safe to drive, or in good resalable condition. Boats must have motors and trailers.

**763 520 0540**
**TOLL FREE 888 440 CARS**
www.courage.org

courage | 75 YEARS
WHERE ABILITIES AND DISABILITIES
BECOME POSSIBILITIES

*Source:* Courage Center.

## Research

Go to your Chamber of Commerce, library, state attorney general's office, or even one of the websites listed in Appendix D to find other nonprofit groups that may fit your criteria. Ask friends and associates for names of organizations with which they have had positive experiences. Learn what you can about the organizations from their annual reports, ratings from watchdog groups, and articles in the press.

You may want to assign a staff person to this task. Do not allow this exercise to go on so long that you have an overwhelming amount of material to consider. Depending on how much money you eventually want to put into your contributions budget, you should have a pool of no more than 20 candidates for partnership.

## Refine

After collecting information on potential charitable partners, contact the executive director or the director of fund development. Tell that person that you are considering the charity for a strategic partnership. You should be specific regarding the terms of the partnership:

- The projected annual donation.
- Whether you want to restrict the donation to a specific project or program area.
- Time limitations (i.e., if you want this partnership to last for one to three years or if you see it as being a much longer-term relationship).
- Any other part of the agreement whereby your company is willing to benefit the charity: volunteers, visibility through company promotions, advertisements, and so on. Ask each charity contacted to respond in writing as to:
    - How this relationship will advance its mission.
    - What it can do to enhance the relationship.
    - Existing strategic charitable partnerships with other businesses.

Invite those groups that best answer your questions to come and visit your office. Better yet, go for a visit at *their* facilities to ensure that their operations reflect what is in their written materials.

## Select and Create the Strategic Alliance

Depending on the chemistry you feel and your strategic goals, you are now ready to select the partner or partners that you will support according to the terms of your agreement. You may want to sign a letter of agreement, particularly if you want this to be an exclusive relationship. As worthy as the cause may be for support from many quarters, you may not want the charity to promote a similar relationship with your competitors.

What might you include in the letter? If your agreement includes workplace giving among your employees, you may want the letter to specify that employees should have the option of being removed from the charity's mailing list that would direct future solic-itations to the home address. If the charity is reluctant to comply with respectful requests of this nature, you should reconsider the relationship *before* it begins.

## Announce

The announcement is a crucial part of your strategy. When done well, it will be key in putting a damper on the flow of requests that clog your mailbox.

Issue a press release in every market where you operate, announcing your strategic philanthropic partnership. You should also ask your charitable partner to issue its own press release. Be clear about what you are doing for the charity, including a dollar goal if you feel comfortable about it. Also, be sure to state the intended duration of the partner-ship. Mention the extent of the exclusive relationship, if you are assigning your complete charitable budget to your partner. If you will still be participating in other charitable activities, mention what they will be (blood drives, United Way, etc.).

Your press release will be a strong warning to fundraisers from other charities that they will be wasting their time approaching your company with requests. Each time your com-pany makes a new donation, issue another release to reinforce the message that you have an ongoing commitment to your partner and that others need not apply. Your charitable partner may be able to provide this kind of service for you through its own public rela-tions staff.

Announce your partnership in your other communication vehicles: annual report, website, newsletters, and so on. Make the information easy to find. Create a link from the company home page to a dedicated page about your partnership. State clearly in the text that you do not consider solicitations from other charities. To further show your commitment to the partnership, establish a link to your partner's website.

Your company does not have to create a formal strategic partnership to be a proactive giver. You can use the first three steps and then simply make contributions to one or two selected charities without any kind of agreement with them. That's how most proactive givers do it.

Unquestionably, there is a lot of work in creating a proactive strategic partnership with a nonprofit group. After all this diversion from your established business activities, you want to be assured that this partnership is going to be worthwhile for your company. Research done at the University of Minnesota and published in the *New York Law School Law Review* says that strategic partnerships are indeed profitable and therefore worth the effort.[1] The research further shows that the more a company spends in charitable expen-ditures, the higher its net income grows.

Becoming a proactive giver does not prevent your company from continuing to give reactively. Proactive giving and strategic partnerships just allow you to budget more accu-rately and give you a substantiated basis for refusing to give when asked by non-preferred charities.

## REACTIVE GIVING

The vast majority of giving is done reactively: you are asked, and you give or you don't give. When you react positively, you get a tax deduction. When you react negatively, you still give but you don't get a tax deduction—the U.S. government decides for you who will get the money.

Hundreds of nonprofit and profit-making institutions benefit from grants and contracts by and with all levels of government. Thousands of college students each year receive Pell Grants to offset the cost of their tuition. If your company hires college graduates, it is likely that you will see some benefit from your involuntary giving to the Pell Grant program.

If your company produces products in the fast-growing biotechnology field, you are probably aware that the National Institutes of Health, the Department of Agriculture, and other federal agencies make grants to all kinds of institutions—businesses as well as nonprofits—for research in this area. Some of those companies may be your competitors. If they are not your competitors today, with the help of those tax-funded federal grants they may be your competitors tomorrow. In this scenario, you may not be too happy about the use of your negative-reactive giving.

My rule of thumb projects 8 to 10 unsolicited requests per week for every 100 employees in your company, regardless of the nature of your business. That can mean a lot of reading for you or whoever is in charge of your program. Therefore, your company's reactive giving program needs to put some structure together so that you can acquire more information about the charities seeking donations, sift out those that are inappropriate, and help you determine which of the remainder will bring the greatest good to everyone involved. Refining the criteria for a positive reaction, and laying them out in an application form or set of written guidelines for grant seekers, will make the job easier for both the charity and your company.

## ESSENTIAL INFORMATION

### Contact Information

The organization should give its legal name and the address of the unit of the organization seeking support, along with telephone, fax, and electronic contact information. It should supply the name of its CEO or executive director and the name and title of the person who is making the request. This may be a professional fundraiser or a volunteer such as your employee or customer.

### Amount of Request

The total amount of the request should be stated. It should also state whether the request is for a one-time gift or a multiyear contribution. In the case of multiyear contributions, the timing and distribution of the payments should be clearly laid out. Your guidelines should indicate the size of donations you will consider.

## Background

Ask for the mission statement of the organization, some of its history, and its legal status. Be sure that each applicant supplies the following important information:

- IRS Tax Ruling 501(c)(3) or 509(A)(1)
- Line-item program budget
- List of Board of Directors/Officers
- Annual report, audited financial statement, and/or statement of cash flow
- Programmatic strengths

## Project Name and Description

Is the organization seeking funds for a specific project (e.g., scholarships, capital improvements), or is the money for general operations? You don't need pages and pages of description to get adequate data on the project. In fact, it is a good idea to state precisely how much information you want or need: two paragraphs or two pages; you decide how much you want to read. If the persons writing the requests cannot get this information into the form you require, then how effective can they be in communicating the rest of their program and mission? After reading the short description, if you feel that you want or need more information, you can always contact them to fill in the blanks.

How does the project relate to your company's priorities and mission? Your company may choose to focus, for example, on K–12 education. The community art museum approaches you for support for a summer program for kids ages 6 through 12. They claim that this is an arts education program. Do you agree? If your company is highly technical, you may be more interested in supporting summer programs that focus on technical skills for that age group. However, if no other summer programs are brought to you for funding, you may want to give this one a second look. After all, many companies employ drafters and commercial artists. Your company might even want to get involved and see if you might help the program director to show the kids various connections between the arts and technology: How is paint produced? What are the physics behind firing a piece of ceramic?

Is there a timetable for the project, or is it a one-time event or program? Even a one-day event project may compare favorably with projects that take place over several weeks or years. If the project has a targeted start and finish dates, keep that in mind when doing your postgrant evaluation.

## Project Impact and Evaluation

How many people will benefit from the project? What kinds of results are anticipated? How does the charity plan to measure the results?

## Plans for Reporting and Communications

The organization should specify how it will report to you on the use of your funds. It also should disclose information on stewardship activities, such as recognition programs, press releases, in-house newsletters, and other print and electronic communication vehicles.

This is one of the areas where charities, especially small nonprofits, fail regularly. When it comes to asking you for money, charities cannot communicate with you often enough. (In fact, the rule of thumb for direct mail is that seven to eleven asks will produce a first contribution, and three to five asks will be needed to produce each subsequent contribution.) After they've got your money, though, depending on the size of the contribution, there are several different scenarios as to what might happen:

- If your donation is less than $250, you may or may not receive a receipt. If your donation is more than $250, the charity is legally obligated to send you a receipt for tax purposes.

- Regardless of the size of your contribution, you may or may not receive a thank-you letter. The smaller your donation, the greater the chance that your letter of thanks will be a form letter or other generic piece of literature, telling you in general some things that are done with donations. It's highly unlikely that this information will relate to the specific project you're supporting, if indeed you are designating your donation.

- Between the time you make your first donation and the next time you receive a solicitation from that group, you may have very little communication in general from the organization and nothing in particular about your project. You may receive an informational newsletter (with a thinly disguised or overt solicitation included) with general information about the charity's program activities, a feature about outstanding donors, and an honor roll of donors. Your company's name will probably appear on the list. In the meantime, you still will not have a very good idea of how your project is progressing.

What's missing here is what business calls *customer service,* and what is called *donor service* or *stewardship* in the nonprofit world. As a businessperson, you know that developing a relationship with your customers is key to keeping their business. Following up on a sale, no matter how small, is important in getting the next, larger order. Your sales staff makes regular phone calls to customers, may drop in on them, and sometimes invites clients for golf, boating, or other outings.

The most important part of this process is assuring that your customer is satisfied with the product or service that you sold. Although charities are not "selling" you a product or service, the principle is the same. To gain your confidence and induce you to "buy" your next piece of their business (that is, make your next donation to a project or program), they need to assure you that you have gotten your money's worth out of your last "purchase" (i.e., that the project/program is proceeding successfully). Without that kind of positive, regular communication, there is little reason for you to have confidence enough in the organization to make a second donation. This reporting, whether on paper or in person, is essential for the next procedural step of your corporate citizenship plan, which is discussed in Chapter 12.

## CHECKLIST

### *Ways of Giving*

❒   Proactive giving

❒   Reactive giving

❒   Strategic alliance

    ❒   Yes

    ❒   No

### *Research Resources*

❒   Chamber of Commerce

❒   Library

❒   Attorney General's office

### *Grant Application Information*

❒   Contact information

❒   Amount of request

❒   501(c)(3) letter

❒   Budget

❒   Directors/officers

❒   Audited statement

❒   Project description

❒   Timetable

❒   Outcomes

❒   Evaluation method

❒   Reporting and communications

## CHAPTER 12

# Assessment

## ASSESSING RESPONSIBLE CHARITIES BEFORE GIVING

When hiring new employees—generally the biggest investments your company makes on a regular basis—you probably have a trial period during which you not only train the new persons, but also assess and evaluate their potential to accomplish the work at a satisfactory level. You most certainly do periodic evaluations of production or service, and an annual review of overall performance.

When your company makes an investment in a piece of equipment, you also evaluate its performance. Does it have a good service record, or did you have to call for repairs far too often? Has the sales representative of the company that sold you the equipment called to follow up and see if you are satisfied? Has the salesperson asked if you have suggestions for ways the manufacturer could improve the equipment to better meet your company's specific needs?

If the answer to these questions is yes, then you would evaluate the equipment and manufacturer or supplier as being satisfactory, good, or even excellent. The next time the sales representative comes to sell an upgrade, you have good reason to be well disposed to buy.

When your company makes a contribution to a charity, you are making a *social* investment. You should want and be able to evaluate the effectiveness of your donation on both the charity's mission and your company's corporate citizenship program mission. If you find that your evaluation of the donation is negative or even neutral, you might think twice about making another grant when you are asked . . . and you are certain to be asked for another grant.

One of the wisest moves you can make to assure that the evaluation will be positive, even before you make the grant, is to be sure that you are giving to a reputable institution. There are many watchdog organizations to help you wade through the sea of requests you'll receive and to bypass some of the confusing financial reports you are likely to see.

## Watchdog Organizations

**BBB Wise Giving Alliance**    The new Better Business Bureau (BBB) Wise Giving Alliance (*www.give.org*) has devised a seal of approval for national charities that meet its high standards. To receive this seal, charities are asked:

- To spend at least 65 percent of total expenses on programs. Exceptions may be given for startup operations.
- That their boards demonstrate proof of adequate oversight for operations and personnel, especially the CEO.
- To allow repeat donors to have their names removed from lists that might be passed along in some way to other groups.
- For biannual written assessments of their performance, including goals and targets for achieving higher effectiveness.

If some of these standards sound familiar, it's because they evolved from the merger of three other watchdog organizations: the Council of Better Business Bureaus Foundation, the BBB Philanthropic Advisory Service, and the National Charities Information Bureau.

The BBB Wise Giving Alliance will be offering its seal to national charities only, such as the American Heart Association or UNICEF. The seal will be valid for two years.

Self-regulating charities associations, such as the Maryland Association of Nonprofit Organizations, have started to issue their own "Seal of Excellence." The Maryland group has set 55 standards in 8 different areas that charities must meet: governance, mission and programs, human resources, finance and legal accountability, conflicts of interest, transparency and disclosure, fundraising, and public affairs and public policy. You may be able to use these, or similar standards issued by an association in your area, to find out about local charities and how they measure up to the Wise Giving Alliance standards.

**GuideStar**    For donors who are oriented toward the World Wide Web, GuideStar offers a charity-screening service called Charity-Guard. The nonprofit organization that operates GuideStar charges clients for screening charity groups; the cost varies depending on the size of the order.

## Doing Your Own Evaluations

Still, many small nonprofits, especially local ones, are off the radar screens of watchdog organizations such as the preceding. Under IRS rules, churches and many other religious organizations, as well as charitable organizations that have less than $25,000 in gross receipts, do not have to file a Form 990, the most commonly scrutinized document. These are highly likely to be the small, community-based organizations that will come to your company for support through your employees or customers.

Whichever areas of philanthropy your company chooses to address, before you give, you must be able to evaluate individual charities to determine that they are not only legitimate, as verified by the available watchdogs, but also ethical. You can ensure this by developing a probing application process so that the charities know that you expect them to respect your rights as a donor. Your application process should incorporate questions and impose requirements to ensure that your donor rights are a priority for the charity.

There is seldom a written contract between a charity and a donor when a contribution is made. Most often, the donor trusts the charities it deals with to be honest, ethical, trustworthy, and confidential. In the absence of some agreement specifically spelling out what a donor expects, unfortunately, charities (both good and bad) often engage in practices that are contrary to a particular donor's intentions and expectations. For these reasons, the Association of Fund Raising Professionals developed the Donor Bill of Rights. Most organizations that employ full- or part-time professional staff encourage their fundraisers to belong to this organization and to adhere to this code of professional ethical standards.

It is incumbent upon donors to verify that the fundraisers they are dealing with are participants in the Donor Bill of Rights program. There are other professional associations for fundraisers. These generally focus on fundraising within a particular sector of the nonprofit world: health and hospitals, religious groups, and so on. Nevertheless, many individuals and companies describe themselves as professional fundraisers without being part of such societies. Be careful. Some may in reality be salespersons, selling a product or service that enhances or supports fundraising, but they are *not* fundraisers and are not bound by the Donor Bill of Rights.

## DONOR BILL OF RIGHTS

This code of conduct asserts that you, as an individual or a corporate donor, have a right:

- To be informed of the organization's mission, of the way it intends to use your grant, and of its capacity to do so effectively.
- To be informed of who serves on its board and their areas of expertise.
- To have access to its most recent financial statements.
- To be assured that your grant will be used for the purpose for which it was made.
- To receive appropriate acknowledgment and recognition.
- To be assured that information will be handled respectfully and confidentially within the law.
- To expect that representatives of the organization will act professionally.
- To be informed whether grant seekers are volunteers, employees of the organization, or hired solicitors.
- To have the opportunity to be removed from shared mailing lists.
- To feel free to ask questions when making a grant and to receive prompt, truthful, and forthright answers.

## Mission and Grant Use Information

There are two ways to receive mission and grant use information: (1) Get a comprehensive application or grant proposal from the organization seeking your support; or (2) become personally involved and familiar with the group. There are pros and cons to both of these approaches.

*Application/Proposal Pros.*    A comprehensive application or grant proposal takes only a little time and small effort on the part of those charged with corporate citizenship tasks in your company. There is little possibility that they will become deeply emotionally biased toward the organization, so they can maintain a high degree of independence in their consideration of requests. That paper application has no holes in the roof, no broken or outdated computers, no eyes that well up with tears to influence your decision or pull you off the track of your strategic giving plan.

*Application/Proposal Cons.*    Only so much information can go into a proposal or application. It cannot describe the intense dedication of staff and volunteers. It cannot demonstrate the actual physical conditions of the facility in question. It's also easy to hide bad news about past program shortcomings.

*Personal Involvement Pros.*    There is nothing like a site visit. When I served on a review panel for the United Way, I was shocked to see that some of the food pantries we visited made little or no effort to disguise the fact that their shelves were bare. They were open for business at that time, and clients were supposed to be able to pick sufficient food off their shelves to make several nutritious meals. The administrators made no excuses for their empty shelves. Needless to say, their funding was not renewed for the next year. The site visit took about two hours and told us all we needed to know for our decision, when coupled with the data on their application.

Better than a site visit is deeper involvement. If one of your company's management team or member of your corporate citizenship committee is on the board of the organization, has benefited from other programs it offers, or works in some other way with the organization, then that person will have an intimate knowledge of its mission and how the mission is accomplished. Clearly, this takes a significant amount of time, but much of it may be voluntary and off company time.

Once you've made a contribution, following up on that first project or program will be a good investment of your company's time when additional requests are made. Follow-up may call for your company's representative to attend an event or make a site visit; again, this takes from two to four hours, depending on the program.

*Personal Involvement Cons.*    Plain and simple, personal involvement is time-consuming. The secondary problem with personal involvement is that it can become personal. Your company representative can develop an inappropriate bias in favor of the organization that clouds his or her judgment when it comes time to make appropriations. It's hard to stay emotionally aloof after seeing the grateful faces of children, the elderly, the sick, and the needy who could all benefit so much from your company's largesse.

## Board Information

A new nonprofit organization once asked me to help it with its fundraising. The cause was related to K-12 education and the board was packed with experts in that field. None of them had experience in fundraising and none wanted to be involved in fundraising. The executive director was at his wit's end; he had no experience in fundraising either. It was obvious that he'd made a mistake in putting together his board.

It's important that nonprofit organizations have representatives on their boards who have expertise in fields directly related to their missions. Health organizations need doctors, nurses, public health professionals, and the like. Social service groups often draw part of their boards from groups of clients or past clients.

The best organizations realize that diversity, in all its connotations and denotations, is important for their boards and the health of their organizations. They need persons with financial expertise to watch over the accountant. They need personnel experts to deal with human resource issues in organizations with hired staff. Legal counsel can be hired, but it's better to have a volunteer attorney on the board.

If the organization addresses an ethnic minority, are there members of that group on the board? Sometimes these people are hard to recruit, especially among immigrant populations. But the success of the organization is closely tied to success in having appropriate board representation from the group.[1]

No matter what the board member brings to the charity in the way of personal professional expertise, it is important that each and every one be committed to helping the fundraising process at some level. This is unquestionably one of the hardest things to determine from reading an application or annual report, but it's not hard to find out during a site visit. All you need do is ask how many board members are donors—and you should get a straight answer. If you don't, then you are not receiving your due under the Donor Bill of Rights.

## Financial Disclosure

Organizations that issue annual reports are most likely to put a very abbreviated summary of the financial statement in it. The trust level of the general public regarding nonprofit management is high, and most people don't even read the financial data. John or Jane Doe is not interested enough or sophisticated enough to recognize what should be included in these reports, and is not educated enough in finance to be able to recognize problems or irregularities.

This is true for most stockholders in the market, too. After the major financial and ethical scandals characterized by Enron, and the periodic outcries against excessive executive compensation, some are starting to look a bit more closely. *Transparency* is a catchword that is heard more often nowadays. Average people, Joe and Jill Stockholder, are looking for information in financial documents that is clear and understandable to them. The same can be said of donors to nonprofits. Each contribution you make is like buying a share in that organization's program.

There is one form that standardizes the financial data of all legitimate 501(c)(3) charities: IRS Form 990. Reading the 990 still requires some education on your part, though.

The federal government requires most nonprofit organizations to file 990s. Those with religious exemptions, and very small organizations that raise less than $25,000 from private sources, do not need to file. There are still many organizations of this kind that are very legitimate.

Neighborhood food and clothing banks are good examples. They often operate out of a volunteer's garage or basement and have informal connections with a church, school, or other community-based institution. Their clients are referred by these same institutions. They operate with a very limited schedule and depend exclusively on volunteers for staffing and all operational and administrative functions. It is when these kinds of groups decide that they must do fundraising to expand that the problem arises in finding out how their finances—their *future* finances, in reality—are to be handled. They have no financial track record, so you must deal with these groups on a trust basis.

Obtaining a Form 990 is not difficult. Those charities that file can send you one in the mail. They are only required to maintain 990 information for the three most recent years, so you cannot easily check back farther if you suspect some past improprieties. The charity can charge you for copies and postage, and is only obliged to send up to four copies in any one year.

GuideStar is the easiest source of Form 990 information, and each charity's form can be found on the GuideStar website in its entirety. Some state attorneys general offer summaries of 990 information for charities in their respective states.

The financial information that likely will interest you the most can be found on pages 1 and 2 of Form 990. For a complete guide to reading the IRS 990, refer to the Minnesota Charities Review Council's "Donor's Guide to IRS Form 990" (*www.crcmn.org/ donorinfo/Form990/index.htm*).

Revenue and expenses are on page 1. This information will address your questions regarding sources of income, net assets, income comparisons over the previous year, use of professional fundraisers, and so on.

On page 2 is information about expenditures: fundraising and management costs internal to the organization, grants to other organizations, and the like. This page tells you what you want to know about the use of the funds from private donors like your company: number of scholarships awarded, equipment purchased, miles of hiking trails cleared.

Important things to watch for while perusing the Form 990 are persistent or increasing operating deficits, or overuse of unrestricted net assets to compensate for budget short-falls. What concerns most donors is the percentage of annual expenses for fundraising and management. The "industry standard" for acceptable levels of non-program expenses is 30 percent. You can determine for yourself if the particular charity you're considering meets the standard by reading and analyzing carefully the figures in the "Revenue, Expenses, and Changes in Net Assets" section of Form 990 Part I.

## Proper Use of Grant

There are dozens of good reasons why a grant might not be used for the purpose intended. Let's say that your company makes a grant to sponsor the opening of a new sculpture garden at the city's art museum. The gala opening should attract a sizeable portion of the museum's membership, a large contingent from the city council, many of the area's prominent citizens, and the like, not to mention a good number of folks from the artistic community. According to the grant proposal, fully a third of all visitors to the sculpture garden for that year should pass through the gates during that opening event. This is wonderful exposure for your company. Much of the event's success, however, depends on an element over which no one has control: the weather. Yes, there is a rain date, but there's no guarantee that Mother Nature will cooperate on that date either.

As luck would have it, there is rain on both days. There is a tent to hold the party-goers so that they can enjoy the wonderful buffet your company is sponsoring. However, as could be expected, the turnout is far below the projections. The impact of your donation has been greatly diminished, and your money is not being used to reach the vast audience you were promised and expected. You must admit that this shortcoming is no fault of the museum, but resolve to support a different kind of project next time — one that is held *inside* the museum.

Money may be diverted for other uses legitimately. For example, a charity approaches your company to underwrite the purchase of a particular kind of computer for an after-school program for handicapped children, at a new location that the charity will be renting. You agree to provide funding for the project as described. After your check has been cashed, the charity notifies you that there has been a change in the program. Instead of holding it at the rented property, the organization has learned that by placing the computers in the public library in some underutilized space, it could save money. It will barter the use of the computers during school hours for rental space in the library after school. No other part of the program changes. This sounds fair; in fact, it sounds better than the original proposal. This is a good diversion of funds.

It is an entirely different story when your money is diverted for different uses without good reason and without your permission. What are some unreasonable diversions?

- Payroll unrelated to the project.
- Cover debts or make up a deficit.
- Support unrelated programs or projects.
- Undertake illegal activities.

The July 15, 2003, issue of the Minneapolis *Star Tribune* carried a story about a local nonprofit organization that was being sued by the city for the return of more than half a million dollars. The city claimed that the money had been used for unauthorized purposes.[2] It's a classic example of the four points in the preceding list. The city alleged that the organization did not keep proper records; that it made a loan to cover the personal expenses of a person uninvolved in the organization and its programs; that it was in chronic debt; and that it held a party that raised no funds, among other possibly illegal improprieties. The cost to the city in pursuing a lawsuit was sizeable, but in times of fiscal hardships, worth the expenditure.

Is *your* company willing to press such a suit to recover its tax-deductible donation? You are entitled by law to request that your money be returned after you have made a donation. But if the charity no longer has the cash or assets to cover it, your company is out of luck. It would also look doubly bad should this information hit the press.

Under no circumstances should a charity use your company's grant for any purpose except the one described in the proposal, unless it notifies you of its intentions. Even then, you should remember that you have the right to ask for your money back. This will nullify your tax deduction, but it also assures you that you are dealing with an honest, ethical institution when you re-grant that same money to another charity or to that same group for a different project in the future.

## Acknowledgment and Recognition

There are businesses and individuals who wish to remain anonymous in their philanthropy. Some are true altruists and philanthropists. They are the ones who sit on the seventh step of Maimonides' ladder of charity.

Donors who allow their philanthropy to be recognized publicly are not always seeking fame and gratitude. They know that by making their gifts public, they are encouraging and challenging others to do the same.

## Confidentiality

There can be a fine line on how the law is interpreted regarding information handling and confidentiality. This is particularly touchy in issues regarding distribution of funds and self-dealing between donors or board members.

A case in point was a disagreement between the University of Minnesota Foundation (UMF) and the Minneapolis *Star Tribune* in the early 1990s. The newspaper's investigative reporters wanted to explore the possibility that some major donors and corporations had been given—willingly or through coercion—undue influence in selecting the persons for endowed professorships. Had this been true, the charitable deduction for the six- and seven-figure donations made to endow these faculty positions would have been disallowed.

The UMF claimed that, as a private, nonprofit organization, it was entitled to maintain the confidentiality of its donor records, including letters, memoranda, and notes to file written by staff and volunteers. The newspaper claimed that the UMF was indistinguishable from the University of Minnesota, a public institution, and was subject to open scrutiny because all but a few of the staff of the UMF were indeed paid employees of the university.

The newspaper won its appeal. Staff at the UMF were disheartened. Although they knew there were no irregularities in any of the documentation (thousands of pages of which had to be photocopied for the reporters), they feared that confidential information about the financial lives of donors, both personal and corporate, could be used for other stories or other purposes by the newspaper. In the end, the story was that there was *no* story. The reporters found no illegal agreements between the donors, the UMF, or the university, and the whole brouhaha died a quiet death. Nevertheless, damage had been done, at least temporarily. Other potential major donors were reluctant to make gifts during the period of the investigation, for fear of having their confidentiality invaded.

## Professionalism

There are stories true, and there are urban myths about the little old lady who changes her will, cutting out her patient relatives to benefit a charity after a fundraiser has wined and dined her and confused her enough to take such a drastic step. Clearly, this is not only unprofessional behavior on the part of the fundraiser; it is plainly unethical. This scenario is unlikely to unfold in most business settings, unless your company is owned by a lonely little old lady.

How do you recognize unprofessional behavior by fundraisers or volunteer solicitors? It's easy: they should be held in conformance with the Donor Bill of Rights. In some of your company's long-term relationships, however, the lines between business relationships and personal ones often become fuzzy. When the charity asks you for special favors, is it taking advantage of you? Is it asking for exceptional discounts for your products or services over a prolonged period of time? Have you allowed it to use your facilities—either your meeting rooms or your phone lines—only to learn that they were not used appropriately?

If your company has been a long-term supporter of the charity, your contact there may be taking your company for granted and overstepping his or her bounds. This is unprofessional. It doesn't mean that you should break off your relationship with the charity; it *does* mean that, as in any business, if an employee is acting inappropriately, a supervisor should be notified. If the person acting unprofessionally is one of the top staff members, contact a board member. For this reason, it is doubly important that you have the list of board contacts, as specified in point 2 of the Donor Bill of Rights.

## Status of Solicitor

**Hired Solicitors**   How often have you been bothered at dinnertime by someone asking for funds for the Sheriff's Safety Council, or the Veteran's Families Funds, or some other unfamiliar charity that seems to be connected with a worthy cause? It's more than likely that the charity is indeed legitimate, but that the person on the other end of the line is a paid telemarketer rather than an employee of the charity. That is, the caller is a commercial solicitor or salesperson.

A report from the California Attorney General's office stated that in 2001, only 38 percent of donations raised by commercial solicitors in that state actually landed in the coffers of the charities that had hired them (see Exhibit 12.1). A full 62 percent went for the charities' fundraising costs and the profits of the hired fundraising companies. Still, that figure was somewhat higher than the 34 percent that charities received in 2000.[3]

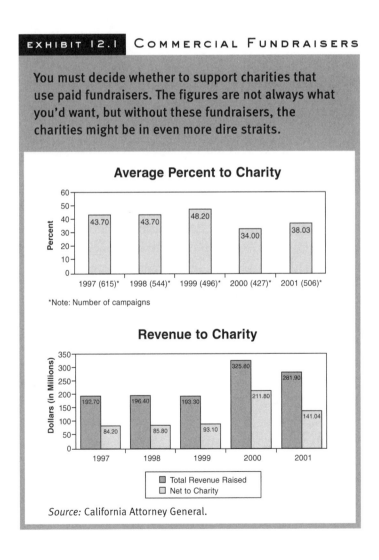

**EXHIBIT 12.1**   COMMERCIAL FUNDRAISERS

You must decide whether to support charities that use paid fundraisers. The figures are not always what you'd want, but without these fundraisers, the charities might be in even more dire straits.

**Average Percent to Charity**

| 1997 (615)* | 1998 (544)* | 1999 (496)* | 2000 (427)* | 2001 (506)* |
|---|---|---|---|---|
| 43.70 | 43.70 | 48.20 | 34.00 | 38.03 |

*Note: Number of campaigns

**Revenue to Charity**

| | 1997 | 1998 | 1999 | 2000 | 2001 |
|---|---|---|---|---|---|
| Total Revenue Raised | 192.70 | 196.40 | 193.30 | 325.80 | 281.90 |
| Net to Charity | 84.20 | 85.80 | 93.10 | 211.80 | 141.04 |

■ Total Revenue Raised
□ Net to Charity

*Source:* California Attorney General.

There's some good to be said for these for-profit fundraising companies. The organizations that hire them generally do not have the kinds of volunteers who are adept at soliciting donations. Sheriffs are more comfortable with arresting people who ask for your money—at gunpoint—than asking for money themselves. Because these organizations have chosen, for whatever reasons, to do their fundraising by telemarketing, commercial solicitors are one of their few options. The organizations are aware that they will receive only a small percentage of the funds raised, and they are satisfied with the arrangement. They are also aware that they are unlikely to get high ratings from watchdog organizations for their fundraising practices, and they are satisfied with that consequence. Their concern is their program, and often they are very good at what they do (working with troubled youth, homeless or disabled veterans, etc.).

**Volunteers**    Generally, the most effective solicitor is a well-trained and experienced volunteer. They are the most credible because they seldom have financial incentives or motives for their association with the charity. Indeed, if they do have such financial connections to the charity, it should raise regulatory and ethical questions about their role in the organization. Even aside from such improprieties, these volunteers are the most trouble for your company because they are often high-level executives whose sole purpose for being invited onto the board of the charity is to raise large gifts from their customers, suppliers, and peers: from you, in other words!

What most often develops over time is a cycle of "I'll scratch your back if you'll scratch mine" or "I'll make a donation to your charity if you'll make a donation to mine." There are two major negative consequences of this scenario. First, getting stuck in this cycle can consume your entire corporate citizenship dollar contribution budget. Second, you may find that little, if any, money given this way goes to charities with missions that fit with your company's strategic goals.

This kind of back-scratching is one of the prime reasons I am called in to work with clients, and is probably one of the reasons you're reading this book. No matter what your relationship is to the volunteer solicitors, as businesspersons they are likely to respect your company's policies regarding donations if those policies are formalized and well articulated. Volunteer solicitors will thus keep their requests to a minimum, particularly if they have to fill out an application.

**Staff**    Once it's clear that some sort of application or grant request must be submitted to your company, in all likelihood it will be handed over to a professional fundraiser. In smaller organizations, staff members play double roles here. The executive director or a program person may do the paperwork. Some small organizations hire free-lance grant writers to do this work. Such persons may specialize in writing corporate grant proposals, foundation grant proposals, or government grant proposals.

In addition to writing the grants, the executive director and/or program person must do significant research on the target of the proposal—*your company*. The object is to craft a proposal that appeals to your sales or marketing strategy. This is fine, as long as you make it clear in a set of guidelines what the company's strategic goals are. Without this, grant writers are likely to go off on tangents that address what *they* perceive as your priorities, and you end up having to read reams of irrelevant materials. This is a waste of your time and a tremendous waste of the charity's resources in paying the grant writer for projects that don't get funded.

Why do charities use these pens-for-hire? Facing up to a real, live, flesh-and-blood prospect is terrifying to most lower-level volunteers and inexperienced staff members. The prospect of face-to-face rejection takes on the aspect of a personal defeat. Anyway, any businesses that are larger than a mom-and-pop shop are viewed as abundant sources of profit waiting to be distributed to the cause. If the organization writes (or has someone write) a grant proposal, no one has to deal with the direct rejection. It comes in a letter, has no face and no voice, and therefore does not bruise the ego.

The professional staff fundraiser is one of the most important parts of any charity's leadership team. Some fundraisers, especially in smaller organizations, are Jacks-and-Jills-of-all-trades. You will encounter them at various levels and in various activities in your interactions with the charity: the fundraiser will ghost-write the direct-mail letters for the executive director or volunteer board chair; she will organize the annual fundraising gala; he will help the long-time volunteer work with an attorney to craft the language for a planned gift, and so on.

As the importance of the paid staff fundraiser has increased, so has the average salary for the position. In higher education, it is not uncommon to find experienced development officers (as they are generally called) bringing in salaries in the low six-figure range. These salaries can be justified by the multimillion-dollar gifts they cultivate and raise by working with donors for year after year, building trust and connections.

Nevertheless, it is difficult for many donors to agree that these staff expenditures are appropriate for nonprofits, especially those in the social service sector. Although many fundraisers are deeply committed to the cause they work for and will accept lower salaries, the majority are professionals like any others. They are looking for an employer who is both a good match for their talents and experience, and is willing to pay the price for what comes with that resume.

## Removal from Contact Lists

The Direct Mail Marketing Association offers a service to remove names from charity mailing lists, as well as lists of other vendors. Some charities make substantial portions of their revenue from selling or renting their mailing lists. If you are willing to have your mailroom deal with junk mail, leaving your company's name on your favored charities' lists will help them in fundraising.

If you have asked to have your company's name removed from a list and you still receive mail obviously generated from it, inform the board chair and withdraw or withhold additional contributions. If all else fails, contact your state's attorney general. Document your process.

## Questions and Answers

This means that you should feel free to ask questions both before *and* after you make a grant. There should be no stalling or evasion. If the charity's representative says that he does not have the answer to the question and that he will get back to you, set a deadline for the response. Hold the organization to that timeline. If you do not get the service you deserve, notify the charity in writing that you are withdrawing your support or your consideration to support because of its failure to provide information.

The questions you ask can either be systematized into an application form, or described in a set of guidelines if all you require is a letter of request. When creating and reading applications, keep your donor rights in mind as much as you do the mission of your company's citizenship plan. Keeping a balance between the two facets of the assessment part of your program is an art, and your ability to maintain that balance will improve with practice.

# DONOR BILL OF RIGHTS CHECKLIST

You have a right:

- ❏ *To be informed of the organization's mission, of the way it intends to use your grant, and of its capacity to do so effectively.*
- ❏ *To be informed of who serves on its board and their areas of expertise.*
- ❏ *To have access to its most recent financial statements.*
- ❏ *To be assured that your grant will be used for the purpose for which it was made.*
- ❏ *To receive appropriate acknowledgment and recognition.*
- ❏ *To be assured that information will be handled respectfully and confidentially within the law.*
- ❏ *To expect that representatives of the organization will act professionally.*
- ❏ *To be informed whether grant seekers are volunteers, employees of the organization, or hired solicitors.*
- ❏ *To have the opportunity to be removed from shared mailing lists.*
- ❏ *To feel free to ask questions when making a grant and to receive prompt, truthful, and forthright answers.*

## CHAPTER 13

# Selecting Grant Recipients

Selection of grant recipients is made easier if you have set out criteria, as described in previous chapters. The first step in the actual selection process is screening.

## SCREENING

Depending on the number of requests you have received since your last distribution, you may only need one person to give an initial screening to the new requests. If there is a need for more than one, the persons assigned to this task ideally should review the requests together for easier consultation.

The first thing they should look at is the postmark on the envelope containing the proposal materials. If it did not arrive at your office by the date you specifically indicated, put it in a "rejects" file. If the organization cannot follow directions well enough to get the request to you on time, it may be an indication of its ability to get projects and programs done on time.

Next, look to see if all the materials you requested, such as the charity's letter of tax exemption, are enclosed; alternatively, they may indicate that you already have it on file. Again, if anything is missing, put the application in a "rejects" file. If the group is unable to provide basic information on the legal or financial status of its institution, it is a telling indication of weak administrative organization, and you should be wary of giving it money.

If your company requires a sign-off on requests by one of your employees, check to see that an appropriate signature is in the appropriate place. Reject those lacking an employee signature.

The final step in the preliminary screening is to see if the organization falls within your company's approved program areas. If your guidelines clearly state that you do not support programs run by houses of worship, and the letterhead says "House of Hope Church," the application can quickly be added to the "rejects" file.

Your company's policy may set a ceiling on the size of grants you make. If a charity is asking for more money than your limit, do not reject the request. Just because it asks for that amount doesn't mean that you are obliged to give 100 percent of the request. Half a loaf is better than none in most cases.

## Evaluating for Grant Decisions

At this point, your pile of requests should be significantly reduced. It is now time for your full committee to address those that made the cut. Each member of the committee should receive a full set of copies of all requests. If you discover that there are so many requests that it is cumbersome to do this, split your committee into two or three subgroups to review and make recommendations on a smaller number of requests each. After following the process outlined in the rest of this chapter, they can then bring their highest-ranked candidates to the whole committee for the final decision.

Your committee may want to create an evaluation worksheet. Having such a worksheet allows committee members more easily to compare apples to apples, with consistent criteria and scales for making decisions. Samples are included in the plans presented in Appendix A.

## Elements of Evaluation

All applications that pass the initial screening should have complete program information, be on time, and contain all required attachments. If for some reason an application without these items makes it past the first screening, the screener—either a member of the committee or a staff person—must be able to justify that decision to the rest of the group.

The rest of your evaluation criteria should correspond to the questions set out in your application or guidelines. You may want to give greater or lesser weight to certain parts of the application, depending on your company's priorities.

### Visibility

Is it of high importance that your company receive significant recognition or visibility as a result of your grant? Has the organization spelled out clearly how it intends to recognize your company and the role it will play in this particular project? Will the charity be doing the publicity through its own in-house vehicles, or does it work with a public relations firm? Has it said it would like to do this, but needs assistance from your publicity department or advertising firm?

### Cost-Benefit Ratio

How much emphasis do you place on the number of people benefiting from the grant? In cases of scholarship awards, clearly the numbers will be small. In contrast, if the charity is requesting that your company provide funds to purchase vans to transport the handicapped to sheltered workshops, you want to know how many people will be accommodated each year for the projected life of the vehicle. When the request is for staff to teach parenting skills to teenagers with babies, it may be optimal to have a smaller ratio of staff to students for good mentoring and clear communication, and larger numbers may be detrimental to the program.

## Replicability

Are you concerned that the project or program is a one-time event that will never be duplicated and therefore will have limited impact on beneficiaries or the community? One-time events have their place, especially if they are fundraising events or donor-cultivation events. One-time events are desirable when a unique situation arises: for example, taking inner-city children to hear or see a presentation from an outstanding personality who is touring the country to inspire children to follow their dreams.

Once a project, program, or event has been completed, the lessons learned from it could be used again, at a much lower cost, as much of the physical, programmatic, and administrative structure is already in place. Support of ongoing programs leverages the dollars your company gives in any one year and amortizes the value of a contribution over the many years of the project's life.

## Your Company's Role as a Donor

Does your company want to take the lead in funding this project? Or are you concerned that the project might fail if the group lacks sufficient support from other donors, either now or in the future? Being the lead donor gives your company higher visibility, but also more risk if other donors cannot be found to enable the charity to do the job right.

## Partners' and Competitors' Participation

Are you sure that other donors to the program are ones with whom you want your company to be associated? Is your competitor also contributing to this project or organization? If so, is this an asset or a liability? Do the other companies with whom you'll share the donor honor roll have reputations as good as your company's, or have they been getting bad press lately?

## Other Community Involvement

What *kinds* of others are involved in this project, as donors or leaders? For instance, if the project is focusing on communities of color, are any minority-owned businesses or persons from that community on the donor list, too?

This point brings to mind a learning experience I had while working at the University of Minnesota on a program to recruit students of color to research careers in the life sciences. The program had been proceeding successfully for several years, thanks in great part to the grants and involvement of the 3M Company and Foundation. One of 3M's employees sat on the advisory board of the sponsoring college. The program had reached a point where the directors wanted to take it to the next level and bring in even more students. We immediately went to 3M to ask for an increase in our annual grant.

3M's management agreed to do so for one more year, but made future increases contingent upon our recruiting persons of color to a special advisory board for the program. They asked, in essence, why should 3M give to this program for communities of color without some strong indication that the local ethnic communities felt it was worth their time, if not their money?

They were absolutely right to insist on this. Once the new corps of advisors was recruited, the program gained a completely new dimension of community involvement and was more successful than ever. What 3M did by being so justifiably demanding was to strengthen the institution.

## Participation of Public Funding Sources

More and more, public institutions are seeking private aid. Will your company be carrying a disproportionate share of a burden that should rightly be carried by government sources?

## Leveraging Your Grant to Meet Challenges

Will your grant be used to meet a challenge issued by another company or donor institution? What is the ratio of the match?

## Geography

Is the organization or the project in the geographic area of principal concern for your company?

## Employee Involvement

If your company wants employee involvement, to what extent is this available in the project? How important is this element, both for the overall success of the project and as compared to other priorities listed in the application or guidelines?

Is it enough for an employee to sign off as a supporter on the application form, or should the employee be required to give some financial support or volunteer effort?

One of the hardest things to evaluate is the match between the organization or the project and your company's philanthropic mission and vision. It is not unthinkable for an organization that has little to do with your mission and vision to have a project that hits the nail exactly on the head. For example, your company guidelines may be very clear that you do not support the arts. Your mission is to encourage literacy. Your corporate citizenship committee receives a proposal from a small theater company that is developing a program focused on improving adult literacy by involving participants in drama. In order for the targets of the program to be in the play, they must be able to read the script. Where do you draw the line? Do you make an exception for this case, or do you expand your mission to take in projects proposed by arts organizations that address literacy, such as this one?

## DOING THE FINAL RECKONING

Taking into consideration the preceding questions, you will create an evaluation form with a grid that allows your corporate citizenship committee members to rate each criterion on a scale of 1–5, 1–3, yes-no, and so on according to the sophistication and complexity of your program. At the top of the page will be the name of the charity, the name of the project (some charities may submit requests for multiple grants, depending on your policies), and the amount requested.

## GIVING WEIGHT TO PRIORITY CRITERIA

How important is one criterion vis-à-vis the others being considered? If program and mission matching is your highest priority, divide your rating system into different sections: The criteria that have greater importance should be rated on a scale of 1–5, while the highest possible rating for less important criteria would be 3.

Each committee member will rank each proposal according to the options on the grid. You must choose a number to cut contenders from consideration. The total of each member's evaluation for each project is added up and the top-scoring proposals are set aside for first consideration.

### Full Funding

The question then is: Do you have enough money to grant the requests in all the top-ranked proposals? If the answer is yes, then you notify your Accounts Payable office of which checks to cut. Send along notes of congratulations to the winners and notes of regrets to the others. Then the committee's job is done until the next deadline. If you have money left over after making those grants, you may want to reconsider your runners-up for funding, or put the money back into funds available for the next round.

## Incomplete Funding

If your budget is insufficient to fulfill all of the grants completely, the committee is faced with three choices:

1.  Give complete funding to some and partial funding to others. What are some of the considerations regarding this option? If your company is the sole donor and you decide to give only partial funding, two things can happen: The project may fail, or the group may be obliged to go out and seek additional support. If the charity is successful, great. It has accomplished its mission *and* expanded its donor base. If it is not successful, a project that you recognized as being worthy of support does not happen and no one receives benefits from it. If, however, your company is only one of numerous prospective donors to the project, your partial fulfillment of the request should only have minor repercussions for the project and its outcome.

    How do you decide which requests should be filled completely and which should receive only partial funding? You will want to look at all the proposals you've approved for funding at some level and give them a second appraisal. If you have time, you may want to ask for additional written information, make a site visit, or ask for a presentation from an organization representative to help you with your decision. If there is not time for such a penetrating examination, review each request with a blank evaluation sheet and see how closely the project and its funding match your evaluation criteria in a new light. You may want to give additional weight to projects that are new initiatives, or ones that the charity has proposed for cofunding with one of your strategic partners. Does one of your top managers sit on its board? Perhaps that will be the straw that tips the scale in favor of full funding.

2.  Give partial funding to all. The question now is how to cut the cake. Should you give everyone who asks a percentage of the total amount requested? Should you vary the amount/percentage according to another formula, perhaps following the same kind of rationale outlined in point 1?

3.  Drop some from the list and distribute more money to those who make the cut. Let's say you have 10 applications. If a passing score for your evaluations is 75 and there are 8 applications with scores between 85 and 100, and 2 others that both made the cut at 75, then it's relatively easy to drop the last 2 in order to completely fund the former 8. However, when you have ten applications and all of their scores are very close, the losers are not so obvious. In that case, refer to the procedure in point 1.

## CHECKLIST

*Screening*

- ☐ On time
- ☐ Materials complete
- ☐ Employee sign-off
- ☐ Fits program criteria

*Elements of Evaluation*

- ☐ Visibility for your company
- ☐ Cost-benefit ratio
- ☐ Replicability
- ☐ Match with your company's donor role priority
- ☐ No participation from your direct competitors
- ☐ Appropriate support from other donor groups
- ☐ Appropriate support from public funding sources
- ☐ Fits geographic criteria
- ☐ Employee involvement

*Funding Options*

- ☐ Complete funding of entire project
- ☐ Complete funding of requested amount
- ☐ Partial funding of some
- ☐ Partial funding of all
- ☐ Drop lower-ranked qualified applications to redistribute available funds among higher-ranked groups

## CHAPTER 14

# Postgrant Evaluation

## EXTERNAL IMPACT

Evaluation should be part of every good corporate citizenship program. For the vast majority of donors, individual and corporate, failure to evaluate the impact of their donations is their program's greatest weakness.

Let's return to the equipment purchase analogy from Chapter 12 for explaining evaluation and take it a bit farther. Virtually every business owns a photocopier and has gone through the experience of buying one or more at least once, so it is an experience to which everyone can relate. Joe, the office machine company salesman, sold your company a photocopier three years ago. It's a great machine: It can print on a variety of papers; it does color, staples, even punches holes! Joe comes by every month to service the machine—often before there's any problem—although lately some of the parts he's had to replace have been costly. He's always asking you how the machine is working for you, asking about improvements you might suggest for future models, and so on. You're happy with the machine, Joe, and the company that makes the machine. The photocopier cost $8,000.

When Joe came by last week, he talked with you about a new photocopier model the company is offering. Not only does it do everything your current machine does, but it takes up less space, can be connected to the Internet for direct download of text and graphics, is more energy efficient, and uses less toner. The price of the machine is $10,000, but it should cost you about $600 less to operate per year.

You evaluate the situation. When Joe sold you the current photocopier, he made promises regarding the machine's operation and maintenance. The actual performance far exceeded your expectations. Your evaluation of the photocopier and the service you've received on it is excellent. Considering that the old machine is starting to require costly repairs, and considering that you have every reason to believe Joe when he tells you that making an investment in the new machine will end up saving your company money, you decide to buy the new photocopier.

The other side of the analogy relates to what happens between you and the representatives of a charity after you have made an $8,000 donation to their cause. In most situations, your company receives an official receipt and a personalized form letter thanking you for your donation. From then on, you are likely to see your name on the donor list printed in the organization's newsletter (if it issues one). Sometimes, there will be an article about the project you're supporting in that newsletter. It's a good-news, feel-good article, but it doesn't give in-depth information. No one calls to invite you to see the project up close, nor do you get detailed written information about what's really happening with your $8,000 donation. When you receive a request for renewal, do you have the same record of performance and service for that "investment" in the organization as you did with Joe and the photocopier, so that you can make an accurate evaluation of the project? Probably not.

If you clearly stated, in your guidelines for grant seekers and in the letter that you issued with the donation check, that you wish to have such complete information, then your donor rights have been violated (see Chapter 12). In this case, the group should receive a low score on an evaluation during your company's annual review of its program, and be disqualified from consideration for future grants. A less drastic step would be to put the charity on notice that a second violation of such rights will result in it being put on a blacklist.

What is essential, if you are to be able to accurately evaluate the results of your grant to an organization, is clear, honest, and timely information from the organization. You must communicate with it at the time you issue the check, if not sooner, as to what your expectations are regarding reporting. If you do not do so and the organization doesn't supply the information, the onus of blame falls on you.

If you do not communicate that you desire this detailed information and the charity supplies it to you anyway, so much the better for your company when you do your evaluation. It reflects even better on the organization because it, like Joe the photocopier salesman, exceeds your expectations and proves itself worthy of future trust and future donations.

Charities that comply with your requests for reports, site visits, and the like should not be given special treatment. They are, after all, just doing what you asked them to do. Your reward to them is keeping them in the pool for consideration the next time they ask for a contribution.

A special word of caution must be given here regarding finances. Although you should already have information about the charity's administrative and fundraising costs from its IRS Form 990 and grant application materials, those data still might be incomplete or misleading. Although experts in the nonprofit field admit that there is no real conspiracy to hide financial facts, many small charities simply don't keep good enough records to accurately distinguish non-program costs. Business donors should therefore determine that the charities they are supporting are capable of giving them the cold, hard cash facts—before writing them checks in the first place.

Overall, the Donor Bill of Rights is an excellent model to use in framing your evaluation criteria. It covers the gamut of issues concerning efficiency, transparency, and accountability that are needed for fair evaluation. Of course, you will want to add in other points that are unique to your company and your corporate citizenship program. For example, if the employees who were involved in the project last year dropped out of it in the middle of the project, why did this happen? What effect did it have on the project, if any? If the organization still is headquartered in your operational area, but the project it is asking you to fund is outside of that area, will you give that project equal priority?

## Internal Impact

This is the question that started this book. Is the money you're giving away to charities making a difference for your companies? How can your company evaluate the impact of your corporate citizenship program? Answering with empirical evidence can be difficult.

Companies of all sizes spend millions of dollars annually in grants and the administration of corporate foundation and citizenship programs. No well-run business would invest this kind of money if there weren't some way to evaluate the benefit coming back to the company itself. Or would they?

Ellen Lugar, director of the General Mills Foundation and Community Action, says that when it comes to giving to charities in the headquarters community, General Mills does not look for a direct relation of charitable giving to the bottom line. She says that the object of such local contributions is to maintain a high quality of life for General Mills employees. In other words, it's a recruitment and retention issue. Because the General Mills program has had such a long life, it would be difficult for the human resources department or General Mills Foundation to measure this point for evaluation on a year-to-year basis. Such a generous philosophy must nevertheless be paying off for General Mills, or else it would have changed strategies years ago.

Is it really possible for a business to measure the direct dollars-and-cents payback to the company for the grants and gifts made to charity? Some internal results are easier to quantify than others, and don't require outside assistance to identify. Employee matching-gift programs and employee volunteerism can be easily measured: just count how many volunteers participate. These kinds of programs are important indicators of employee morale and commitment to the company.

For those whose objectives are not so easily measured, the Contributions Academy (*www.contributionsacademy.com*), a South Carolina-based educational consulting group, offers some interesting guidelines. Curt Weeden, Contributions Academy president, makes two strong recommendations to help businesses measure corporate citizenship's impact on the bottom line:

1. Know what it is that you want measured. Is your measurable outcome employee recruitment and retention, as Lugar's unspoken agenda suggests for General Mills? Are you using the program to help the company achieve success in a new market?

To identify these areas easily, you should refer to the mission and vision statements of your company's corporate citizenship program. If you cannot identify measurable outcomes in that section, consider rewriting the statements so that your measurable goals will be clear.

2. Develop the terms of measurement. Will you do the measurement on a department-by-department basis, with Human Resources measuring the factors that relate to its arena and Marketing doing the same in its bailiwick? Should each department devise its own evaluation instrument, or will you want certain parts of the instrument to be uniform?

As in any campaign, results are seldom visible or measurable on the basis of one year's operational data. Do you want to conduct these measurements annually, or on a more extended schedule (say, every three or four years)?

If you are supporting a variety of programs, how can you determine their relative effects on your company if you are also seeking to achieve multiple internal outcomes? In other words, is it really the employee matching-gift program that's helping retention, or is it the company-wide, summer-long volunteer program that's making more of an impact?

If your corporate citizenship program is part of a multilayered effort to enter a new market or sell a new product, it will be difficult to determine the amount of influence it has had on the success or failure of the marketing campaign.

Unless your company has in-house experts to do this evaluation, you must seek assistance. According to Weeden, an important part of doing successful evaluations is finding the right partners to cooperate in measuring.

The first partner is the nonprofit grantee. If your company seeks higher visibility, your charitable partner should find it easy to provide proof for evaluation. It can demonstrate the amount of visibility it has generated for you by providing you with plaques and certificates, copies of news clips from newsletters and articles, listings in programs and announcements, and the like. It will invite your representatives to events where the company will be acknowledged publicly. Your evaluation team can simply make a note of each mention, or go farther and break down mentions by category: news story, advertisement acknowledgment, published photograph, name in program, and so on.

Companies that adhere to the Baldrige Award criteria for total quality management, as promoted by the National Institute of Standards and Technology (NIST) and state Council for Quality chapters, subject their grants programs to the same stringent examinations done on the rest of their operations. When adequate attention is given to the quality of corporate citizenship, such as assigning sufficient staff to supervise and administer it, the effort adds to the excellence of the company's composite performance. According to the study issued to the press and online in May 2003 by the Baldrige Awards Program at NIST, for eight of the nine years from 1995 to 2003, companies receiving Baldrige Awards outperformed the S&P 500 by up to 6:1.[1] Corporate citizenship is only one of the criteria for the Baldrige Award, but it cannot be ignored in the equation for success (see Exhibit 14.1).

Larger companies often call on independent evaluators as partners to determine a grant's internal effectiveness. Independent evaluators can be faculty or staff of colleges and universities with business schools, or they can be private firms. Nonprofit sources, such as the Committee to Encourage Corporate Contributions (*www.corphilanthropy.org*) and Business for Social Responsibility (*www.bsr.org*), also offer guidance for evaluating internal effectiveness. In 2002, the Committee to Encourage Corporate Philanthropy (CECP) began its "Building the Measures" initiative.[2] Leaders from 21 of the top U.S. companies, such as Cisco Systems and Bank of America, are attempting to create a common standard by which the corporate world can measure the amount and impact of its community involvement efforts nationally and globally.

Business for Social Responsibility offers its members information through its publications and through training courses. Both BSR and CECP are membership organizations,

---

**EXHIBIT 14.1** **QUALITY CARING**

**Performing your company's social responsibility can be made easier if you participate through programs sponsored by industry associations.**

**AMERICAN SOCIETY FOR QUALITY**

The role of community advocate is one that ASQ takes very seriously. In order to highlight the potential of quality to benefit humanity, ASQ has launched the Community Good Works Program, providing matching grants and knowledge transfer to improve local communities and create a body of evidence that documents the efficacy of quality.

Candidates for matching grants include not-for-profit, community-based, or community-serving organizations with 501(c)(3) tax-exempt status. Local government agencies are also acceptable.

To learn more about ASQ's Community Good Works Program please visit our Web site at **www.asq.org/goodworks/**.

**American Society for Quality**

**ASQ**

*A 108,000 member-strong professional association committed to promoting community excellence through the use of quality tools and techniques.*

*Source:* Copyright 2003 American Society for Quality. Reproduced with permission.

but they are not the only ones that address corporate citizenship. Yes, it will cost precious budget funds to join, but you must weigh the benefits of membership against the cost of hiring a consultant if you want to do effective evaluation.

Most experts in the field agree, like General Mills, that the real benefit of corporate citizenship cannot be reduced to bottom-line figures. The fact that so many companies are deeply involved in these activities shows that the biggest benefit to the company, no matter how you evaluate them all, is the satisfaction of being a responsible member of the greater community.

## Checklist

### Terms of Measurement: Internal

- ❑ Company-wide assessment and tool
- ❑ Department-by-department assessment and tool

### Timing

- ❑ Annual assessment
- ❑ Periodic assessment

### Evaluation of Grant Performance/Effectiveness

- ❑ Nonprofit provided reports or other evidence of project execution
- ❑ Nonprofit complied with requests for recognition/anonymity
- ❑ Project completed on time
- ❑ Project completed on budget

## CHAPTER 15

# Celebrations and Publicity

Without a plan to create or take advantage of recognition for your company's good works, you may be in a position to ask the ancient Buddhist question, "What is the sound of one hand clapping?" To make the loudest noise, your company's plan should call for your public relations operation to be the right hand, and the staff of the charities you support to be the left hand.

## THE RIGHT HAND: YOUR COMPANY'S EFFORTS

If your company is relatively small, you may think it's unnecessary to do any internal promotion about what the corporate citizenship program is accomplishing, and believe that word-of-mouth should suffice to get the news out. This is a fallacy. Most people are at work to earn a living and then get on with their private interests. You must be proactive in getting the attention of your employees and shareholders, so that they will know and understand what the company's citizenship program is and does.

### In-House Communication

If communication between spouses—who live in the same house—is difficult enough in these days of two-income households, can we assume that people who have the same employer but work in different buildings or locations will get information by word-of-mouth? Just as spouses from time to time need to plan a night out together so that they can talk without distractions, so does your business need to create tools to deliver clear messages to employees about the company's citizenship program.

**Paper and Electronic Newsletters/Bulletin Boards**   If your company already has a newsletter or bulletin board, it is, of course, most logical and practical to use these existing means of communication. Adding a monthly or periodic section to it about the company's citizenship activities will bring the program to the attention of those who read it.

What about those who don't? How do you get *their* attention? To answer those questions, you must ask *why* they're not paying attention. Is there a language barrier? Although English is the general language of instruction, and the most commonly used language in the United States, there is no official language for our country, and millions of workers don't speak or read English well. Digesting the material and communicating the abbreviated message in other languages will allow those workers to know what's happening.

Are they not paying attention because they think this is not something that concerns them and their immediate coworkers? To address this situation, be sure that articles and announcements include information, names, and pictures of employees at *all* company levels. We all know the excitement of seeing our names in print and sharing this recognition with those around us.

**Promotional Materials**   Your company produces brochures and has a website to tell prospective customers and investors about the company, its products, and services. These are not, strictly speaking, internal communications, but they are materials you produce in-house or distribute directly from inside.

You may already include in such materials the logos of, or information about, business and trade associations the company belongs to, such as the Better Business Bureau, the Chamber of Commerce, or, for example, the State Builders Association. Why not put the logo of your most prominent charitable partner on your materials, too? It sends a positive message about your corporate citizenship, is good publicity for the charity, and as a corollary invites readers to do the same with their companies' materials.

**Annual Reports**   Private companies do not need to issue annual reports, but public ones do, and often allocate a sizeable portion of their budget to making it look impressive to current and potential investors. As relatively few shareholders generally attend the company's annual meeting, the annual report is management's most valuable means of communicating important messages to this audience. It is the vehicle you will use to tell about and justify your company's charitable allocations.

When the amount, both in terms of actual dollars and percentage of profits, is small, shareholders are unlikely to question how money is given to charities. When the totals start getting into five and six figures, though, conflicts and misunderstandings can arise. For example, in 2003, Warren Buffett announced a change in the way Berkshire-Hathaway would be handling its philanthropy.[1] Several years earlier, he had instituted a system whereby most of his shareholders could designate where company donations would go. Some of them took advantage of this opportunity to have the corporation make sizeable donations to charities with missions that were contrary to Buffett's personal and political interests. Buffett's power within the corporation allowed him to change the system to prevent this from happening in the future.

The annual report is management's once-a-year opportunity to explain and justify the company's corporate citizenship vision, mission, philosophy, administration, activities, and results. Print the vision and mission statements in the annual report so that there is no question as to what you are trying to accomplish. When shareholders see the program as making social investments that have positive outcomes for the company's bottom line, they will endorse it.

Use the corporate citizenship program section of the annual report to highlight its effects on *people*. Reproduce a letter from last year's scholarship students, telling about their experiences on campus. Put a crayon drawing done by one of the kiddies in the homeless shelter on the title page of the corporate citizenship section of the report. Use a photo of your employee and her children in their company tee-shirts to illustrate a report on their efforts in raising funds to combat a disease suffered by a coworker. These are only a few ways to provide testimonials to report to readers about the effectiveness of your program.

**Events**    Written and electronic communications are not the only way to get the message across. Announcements made at the company picnic or the shareholder annual meeting will reach additional internal stakeholders.

Events can be simple or elaborate, depending on your budget and the impression you want to make. If yours is a smaller company, combining a celebration of your company's citizenship activities with an existing event might make sense. If you have a company picnic, invite your scholarship winners and their parents to join your employees at the festivities. When recognizing staff with employment anniversary awards at your semiannual sales training meeting, recognize the employees who have volunteered 50 hours that year to your charitable partner. Present a plaque or gift certificate to the winner of the interdepartmental fundraising competition. These kinds of events also produce great stories and photos for your company newsletter.

Companies with larger budgets can turn these celebrations into newsworthy events. Videos depicting the company's involvement with different charities can be used for display on a big screen at the event and then be webcast to employees at off-site locations.

The same kinds of testimonials (from winners, participants, and recipients) that bring emotional and personal validity to a company picnic can evoke the same reaction with a larger crowd when the person is up on a stage at your shareholder annual meeting. Picture a scholarship winner standing there with a backdrop of your company's logo and the seal of the Ivy League school this student is attending. The blend of the student's gratitude with your company's pride in supporting such a talented youth will saturate the atmosphere at the event.

Make sure that you invite a reporter from the student's home community to attend the event, or at least send a press release and photo to the editor. Such "home-towners" are the bread-and-butter of the press in smaller communities and get good placement.

Use still photos, film, video footage, or audiotape of your event in new advertisements about your company. Include other parts of such material in recruitment packages for new employees. The bigger the event, the more material there will be for you to use throughout your operations.

## External Communication

As much as you might want your nonprofit partner to do publicity regarding your support of its programs, this is not something you can always count on them to do as you'd like. You think that your company's contributions deserve a certain level of publicity, but it may have a lower priority on the charity's donor stewardship list. You expect things to happen quickly, but it may take time for a nonprofit organization with a small staff (all of whom are doing multiple tasks) to get around to issuing announcements. For these and a host of other reasons, you can take the initiative and do your own publicity.

**Press Releases**   Let's go back to our analogy about communication between spouses: Even when communication between two marriage partners is good, there are times when these individuals need or want to communicate publicly with a clear and consistent message. We are all familiar with the photos of happy couples in newspapers, announcing engagements and marriages. Many community newspapers carry birth announcements. These are happy occasions and we want everyone to know about them in print.

When your company gets a new client or renews a major contract, you already may send out press releases. Just like a marriage or birth, it's good news that you want your community to know about. It makes your company look successful, and success breeds success. If your company has good news about a successful charity project you're undertaking or that you've recently completed, then that, too, is good news and deserves announcing.

A published press release does four things:

1.  It gets your story out cheaply. If you have an in-house staff person write and distribute the story, it costs virtually nothing. Even if you do not have a company employee regularly assigned to this, by applying a simple formula to your situation you can create a release that should be adequate to gain the attention of an editor.

    What is the formula? Use a piece of your company's letterhead. On the left-hand side, at the top, type "Press Release"; below it, type "For release" and then the earliest date when the article can be printed. Opposite those words, print "Contact"; below that, type the name and telephone number or email address of the staff member who is in charge of communications or the corporate citizenship program.

    The information in the press release follows the standard for all news stories:

    - *Who.* The *who,* of course, is your company. The *who* also is either your company's CEO or another person involved in the company's corporate citizenship program activities or administration. The more names you give, the better. Be sure to identify each person by his or her title.

    - *What. What* is the fact that your company has made a major donation of dollars or in-kind goods to a particular charity.

- *Where. Where* can be the location of the company or the place where the announcement was made. If your company is contributing toward the YMCA Camp's campaign to build a new outdoor amphitheater, it's a good idea to make the announcement at the camp on the site of the future structure.

- *When.* Give the date of the actual announcement. Also give information about the timing of the project. You may announce your company's exclusive corporate underwriting of a walk-a-thon for cancer research, even though the event itself may not take place for months to come.

- *Why.* This is where your company's written policies and procedures come in handy. You can explain the rationale behind the support you are giving the charity in terms of what your company wishes to accomplish in the community; you can also stress the worthiness of this particular program or project to be your instrument to accomplish your goals.

- *How.* Explaining *how* the project works will give the nonprofit a chance for additional visibility. Explaining *how* your company is involved (employee volunteers, management serving on the charity's board, etc.) gives additional positive exposure to your company and its employees as good citizens.

2. It tells the public that your company is profitable enough to be making substantial charitable donations. If your company is public, it sends a message that this company is a good one in which to invest. Remember what research showed us in Chapter 1: Companies with good giving programs showed an appreciably higher three-year return than companies without them.

3. It tells the public that your company is a good citizen. It reinforces the unwritten messages that this is a company whose products and services they want to buy; this is a company that they may want to work for; this is a business they want to have located in their community.

4. It gives your charitable partner additional exposure. After all, this is part of your charitable mission: to improve your community by supporting work done by nonprofit organizations. Putting out a press release is another way of giving support, particularly if the organization is small and does not have staff to produce regular press releases of its own. When other potential donors, both businesses and private individuals, see that your company is supporting the charity, it gives the group greater credibility and enhances the organization's fundraising potential.

**Paid Advertising**    Press releases are great because they take little effort and are very inexpensive. Press releases aren't great because there's absolutely no guarantee that they will be published. When you want to get the word out to the public about your achievements as a good corporate citizen, you can make your advertising budget do double duty for you by using advertising to promote your corporate citizenship program.

Many publishers offer discounted rates for charities that advertise in their publications. This will not be the case for you, no matter how prominently your charitable partner appears in the ad. However, you can take two approaches to creating your advertisement to make the most of the advertising budget expended for it.

First, you can invest in a sophisticated advertisement that can be used in several formats. What are some of the uses? The ad can run in the local popular press as well as your local business press or national or state industry publications. With only minor changes, the same ad can be used in promotional materials for your company, and then again in the company's annual or quarterly report to shareholders (see Exhibit 15.1). Because the advertisement shows a high level of sophistication, it imparts an image of high quality to your organization, something that you want particularly for marketing to an upscale audience who might use highly specialized services.

Second, you can do something more modest. Reproducing testimonial materials received from charities is inexpensive, and it leaves no room for doubt as to the validity of your claims of doing good in the community. It gives an image that your company would rather spend its money to help the community than spend it on creating flashy advertisements. It says that this company is out to save money for itself and make good social investments. Extending the message, it says that this company is out to save money for *your company.*

**Airways Advertising**    Just as you can build information about your company's corporate citizenship into your print advertising, you can build it into television and radio advertising. There are two ways of doing that as well.

1.  *Paid Advertising.* Adding a tag line to your regular advertising gets the word out before you actually give. "During the month of June, with every purchase of 20 widgets, Your Company will donate a portion of the profits to the Community Charity Name!" This kind of announcement drives sales to your company and gives a good impression to the audience.

    You can also tell your story after the fact. "During the month of June, Your Company donated $1,000 to the Community Charity Name, thanks to the support of our customers!" This makes your customers feel great and keeps them coming back to your business. Neither of these takes more than a few seconds out of your 30- or 60-second airtime.

2.  *Public Broadcasting.* The second way of doing airways advertising is with public television and radio stations. This kind of advertising is actually considered an underwriting grant, and can be budgeted with the rest of your corporate citizenship activities.

    Even though you are supporting public broadcasting, nothing prevents you from using those announcements both to tell something about your company's products and services, and also to tell more about the other charitable activities you are undertaking. It's not unusual to hear a lead-in program announcement

**EXHIBIT 15.1** Tooting Your Own Horn

You can notify your customers that you are thanking them with a donation to charity. This can be done by sending a note in the mail, or more publicly by buying an ad in an appropriate publication. In either case, it gets the message out about your company's community values.

*Dear Customer,*
*Since 1984, your support has enabled us to provide free calling to many of the Homeless at many Salvation Army Locations in Minnesota, Colorado, and Arizona. Once again—for the eighteenth year in a row—on Thanksgiving Day and Christmas, POPP Telecom, on your behalf, will help the Homeless call their families.*

**Thank you for your business—from all of us at POPP Telecom**

---

Star Tribune/Joe Kimball
Published Friday, November 26, 1999

**Around St. Paul: Homeless give thanks for long-distance calls**

Some of St. Paul's homeless people got an early Thanksgiving feast at 8 a.m. Wednesday at the Salvation Army's Citadel Corps and Community Center at 410 W. 7th St. Volunteers served turkey, mashed potatoes, stuffing, and pumpkin pie to 199 people. No one complained about the early hour for the hearty feast. The center provides a daily breakfast, less elaborate than this, for those down on their luck.

After Wednesday's feast, a dozen guests made free long-distance calls, courtesy of Popp Telecom of Golden Valley.

"There were calls to South Dakota and Mankato, and one man tried Havana, Cuba, but didn't get through. Another person wanted to call Cambodia, but didn't have the right number," said Jennifer Wurm, emergency programs director at the St. Paul Salvation Army. "The callers who got through were very happy, some said they hadn't talked to the other person in months," she said.

---

THE SALVATION ARMY
Founded in 1865 by William Booth
NORTHERN DIVISION
2300 Freeway Boulevard, Brooklyn Center, MN 55430-1793
Phone: 612-566-2040   Fax: 612-566-8954

February 3, 2000

Mr. Bill Popp
620 Mendelssohn Ave.
Golden Valley, MN 55427

RE: The Popp Telecom Phone Home Project

Dear Mr. Popp:

The Salvation Army offers hope and healing to hurting and needy in the community. A warm meal and a safe place to sleep, a listening ear or a whispered prayer are hallmarks of our mission. Incorporate the opportunity to reunite with estranged loved ones during the holiday, and a new dimension of healing is added.

Thanks to Popp Telecom Phone Home Project families are reunited and bridges are built. On Thanksgiving and Christmas day, clients at The Salvation Army are able to make free long distance phone calls to family and friends. This project can lift the burden of a heavy heart.

"The less fortunate are no less deserving of what we all take for granted," says Captain Steve Woodard, administrator of The Salvation Army Harbor Light Multi-Service Center downtown Minneapolis. "The Phone Home Project is a blessing. I am moved each time I hear someone speak to a daughter, son or mother and father for the first time in years." During a phone call it can be easier to reach out and begin a healing process, Woodard says. "There is an opportunity for relationships to begin to mend and hope for the future."

Offering hope and a future is a goal of The Salvation Army. Thanks to community partners like Popp Telecom, it is a goal with a future.

Sincerely,

Lt. Colonel David E. Grindle
DIVISIONAL COMMANDER

---

**POPP**®

*TELECOM*
**The Best ~ In Many Ways**

Voice, Data, Internet Networks

**TOSHIBA** Telephone Systems

Professional Optimistic Prepared People

763-797-7900    •    1-800-234-POPP (7677)    •    www.popp.com

*Source:* Popp Telecom. Reproduced with permission.

that says something like, "The Classical Hour is made possible by the generous underwriting support of Your Company, who invite our listeners to join their employees as they work with Riverwatchers of the Mississippi Valley to clean up the shoreline on July 5." This sends an additional message (for the same donation) about the range of community concerns your company is addressing.

There are some disadvantages. Your airtime will likely be much less than what you would get with a commercial advertisement. Your message will not be as informational as with a commercial ad. For example, you probably will not have the opportunity to advertise special sales or promotional offers. "Your Bank is offering the highest rates on certificates of deposit in town" is *not* an acceptable message for this kind of nonprofit advertising, even though it *may* be a message you really want to communicate.

Charities like to thank their generous, consistent donors in public ways. They, too, want to get multiple uses out of their advertising, marketing, and donor stewardship budgets.

Many charities do this by ending their campaigns with a purchase of ad space in appropriate publications, acknowledging one or more donors for their contributions. Depending on how the charity decides to structure the thank-you campaign, your company's name can be just one on a list of corporate donors, or you might be singled out to receive special attention. In either case, it is free advertising in a very positive light.

No matter what you do to toot your own horn, be careful not to be overly self-congratulatory or to distort the actual impact of your corporate citizenship. People will notice, and it can backfire on you. One of the most visible examples of the boomerang effect of excessive self-promotion was the series of *Doonesbury* comic strips published by cartoonist Gary Trudeau during 2000 and continuing from time to time into the present. The target of his sarcastic humor was the Philip Morris Company, now called Altria. Philip Morris, with a bad image as a tobacco merchant, attempted to redirect attention from its tobacco products to its Kraft Foods division through a series of ads showcasing Kraft's activities with food banks for the needy. This unquestionably was a fine effort by Philip Morris to demonstrate its good corporate citizenship, and indeed Kraft's donations were real and noteworthy. Nevertheless, *Doonesbury's* comic character, Mr. Butts—a walking, talking cigarette—appeared regularly to alert readers to what Trudeau viewed as Philip Morris's attempt to "blow smoke" over the issue of the dangers of cigarette smoking. And his campaign was highly successful. The public did not change its negative opinion of Philip Morris.

The story doesn't end there. The company received even more negative publicity when Philip Morris USA was exposed as having spent $100 million in 1999 to tell the public about its good works—which totaled just $95 million.[2]

The public will recognize untrue or misrepresented information about corporate citizenship. The press thrives on uncovering such stories. The July 14, 2003, issue of the

Minneapolis *Star Tribune* carried a major story on how highly publicized charity events involving members of the Minnesota Vikings football team actually netted very little for the charity while providing major goodwill visibility for the players. The resentment against highly paid athletes could only grow worse after exposure of such self-serving activities.[3]

Toot your own horn, but pay attention to what's printed on your sheet music, and be sure you don't hit a sour note.

## The Left Hand: Recognition from Your Charitable Partners

Much of this has been discussed in previous chapters, but there is more detail to be covered. The minimum recognition you can expect from the nonprofits that you are supporting is to be listed in their in-house vehicles as a donor: an honor roll in their newsletter or event program, a plaque at their facility, or the like. Though this is not really public recognition, your name will be visible to those who receive the publications, visit the organizations' offices, or attend their events.

### Testimonials and Awards from the Charity

Another step up on the ladder of donor recognition is when the nonprofit presents your company with a certificate, plaque, or other testimonial. This is something you can hang in your lobby or meeting area for your customers and suppliers to see, giving continuous (though unspoken) praise for your company's good works. It is also a constant reminder to your employees about the charity's appreciation of your company's philanthropy.

It is easiest for the charity to simply mail you these testimonials. Don't settle for that. Request that a representative of the organization deliver the plaque in person and make it a special event for the company employees. If the charity does not have a local representative who can drive over to your plant on short notice, it is worth waiting to make the presentation until one of its staff members comes to your town. That makes the award event more newsworthy.

When I worked for CARE, its offices were in New York City. CARE had been receiving substantial donations for many years from an employee group at the General Electric Research and Development Division in Schenectady. When their accumulated donations reached a point where we realized that it would be very poor donor stewardship not to make a testimonial presentation in person, I drove up the Hudson Valley for a visit.

GE arranged for nearly the entire staff to be present in the cafeteria for the award ceremony. When I finished with my speech, several employees stepped forward to tell their stories of how they had been displaced persons after World War II and how the CARE packages they received had saved their lives. The Schenectady newspaper did a front-page story on the event, profiling the GE employees. For weeks afterward, we saw a notable peak in our new contributions from Mohawk Valley towns served by that newspaper.

Designate a wall or install a trophy case for these awards. Your company may already have a similar display area for your patents or industry awards, so you can simply expand it. Use this same area to recognize your employees who have done outstanding work with the company's charitable partners, or whatever volunteer activity your company has approved as part of its program. Whether you change the case monthly or annually, or even if you just add another name to a plaque or list, it will be a source of pride for that employee among the rest of your staff.

If your company has multiple locations, don't hoard your testimonials at headquarters. Circulate them among all your locations, and have a small celebration when an award arrives at a new location, just as if it were a sports trophy. Those employees in Podunk worked hard to make the company profits that were subsequently donated to charity. They may also have added their own money to the company campaign funds that were donated to the charity. Be sure to recognize their role in bringing that award to the company.

## Press Releases

Your company can send out its own press releases about these awards, but, as mentioned earlier, there is no guarantee that they will be printed. Encourage your charitable partners to issue their own press releases. They are likely to cover the story from a much different angle that might be more appealing to the editor. Ask to see the text before the story is sent to the media to make sure that all the facts about your company are accurate. If the organization honoring your company is the local affiliate of a national group, urge your contact to push the story "upstairs" so that it can get exposure to a larger audience with connections to the charity.

## Events

Many charities hold annual donor recognition and gratitude events. Sometimes they are complimentary and sometimes there is a nominal fee for the banquet. Go to all of them, whether or not your company will be in the spotlight.

Why? First of all, you will learn more about the organization. These donor recognition events are meant to be educational and to reinforce your decision to support the charity. Second, they are excellent opportunities for networking. Be sure to ask to be put at a table with people you don't know, rather than with the supplier you see every day. Third, nobody insists that *you* go to every event. Share the opportunity with others in your company. You can make your selection based on involvement with the charity or participation in the corporate citizenship committee. It may also be a good way to reward people for service to the company in other ways, because . . . Fourth, these events are generally fun!

## Recognition from Third Parties

The philanthropic community likes to congratulate itself. We have already discussed the Keystone Program found in many communities, which is a recognition society for companies that give between 2 and 5 percent of pretax profits to charity. There are numerous other awards offered to recognize companies for good citizenship.

The professional fundraisers who work so hard to part you and your money have an excellent vantage point from which to view the donor world. Their professional society, the Association of Fundraising Professionals (AFP), sponsors an annual Philanthropy Day on a geographic chapter level to provide members with continuing education and to recognize the outstanding donors in their area.

You can piggy-back on awards given to charities you've supported. The Mutual of America Community Partnership Award, offered by the Mutual of America Foundation, was created to recognize nonprofits that do an outstanding job of bringing together resources from the public, private, and social services sectors for the greater good of the community. The award consists of a cash prize and a professionally produced video of the project—the one *your company* helped to create.

If your company's corporate citizenship program is well planned and well conducted, you will likely end up funding some highly creative projects in innovative ways. The Council on Foundations offers the Robert W. Scrivner Award for Creative Grantmaking. Past recipients include the president of the IBM International Foundation, who was also vice president of IBM's corporate-community relations program.

The Council on Foundations also honors excellence in communications by grant makers. Among the winners of its Wilmer Shields Rich Awards for Excellence in Communications in 2000 was Pittsburgh's Columbia Gas. The utility organized a campaign, which included billing envelope inserts, advertisements, and classroom materials, to promote the performing arts in the community. As a result of the campaign, local arts groups saw a visible increase in attendance by people who took advantage of the special offers made during the campaign.

The Better Business Bureau sponsors Integrity Awards and opens the nominations to the general public. When your company has a comprehensive corporate citizenship program that combines volunteerism, cash gifts, and in-kind donations, along with ethical investing and the like, it is a strong contender for this kind of honor.

Don't hesitate to nominate yourself for these awards when possible, or to approach a fundraiser with whom you've worked about nominating your company. You know you deserve it, and the old saying is true: The squeaky wheel gets the grease.

## CHECKLIST

### *In-House Activities and Communications*

- ☐ Paper and electronic newsletters/bulletin boards
- ☐ Trophy case/wall of fame
- ☐ Promotional materials
- ☐ Annual report
- ☐ Events

### *External Activities and Communications*

- ☐ Press releases
- ☐ Paid advertising

### *Recognition from Grantee Organizations*

- ☐ Plaques, certificates, other tokens
- ☐ In-person presentations
- ☐ Press releases
- ☐ Invitations to events

### *Third-Party Recognition*

- ☐ Industry awards
- ☐ Philanthropic institutions

## CHAPTER 16

# Review and Revision

Congratulations. You've read through this book and you've instituted your program. A common question I'm asked at this point in the process is, "Can we make changes?" Of course you can—it's YOUR money! In fact, the best programs make it policy to review and revise on a regular basis, either biennially or every five years.

Some companies change the focus of their giving regularly. Northwest Airlines has a different beneficiary for its donated frequent-flyer miles every quarter. It knows that some charities have greater appeal to the wide variety of its customers than others. The General Mills Foundation regularly evaluates the effects of its giving and refocuses the program when specific goals are met.

One of the benefits of having a simple corporate citizenship program, where grants are made from current profits rather than a company foundation, is the simplicity of changing policies and procedures. Depending on how you structure your decision-making process and your committee membership, making changes can be as simple as having your company president or committee chair issue an executive order.

## REVIEW

Review should be a regular part of your program. There are two parts of review:

1. *Reviewing the effects of the program on your company's internal goals.* If you discover that virtually none of your employees are taking advantage of a highly promoted employee-matching gift program, which was intended to improve retention, something should be done about it.

2. *Reviewing the effects of the program on your external goals.* Although maintaining a high quality of life in your headquarters community is a never-ending job, gather the evidence that your company has done a great job in supporting the arts, recreation, health, and education.

## REVISION

Let's look at some ways to revise these two scenarios.

- Revision of the policy about employee matching gifts might be in order. You might want to make it more appealing by expanding the kinds of charities that are eligible for a match, or increasing the match ratio from 1:1 to 2:1. If those strategies don't work, then at the next review you may choose to save the administrative costs of the program by terminating it and directing those dollars to another, more popular part of the corporate citizenship program.

- When another major employer in the area begins to share the quality-of-life burden in a big way (say, by building a wing on the hospital or renovating playgrounds), you may feel that this mission can be downgraded to a lower priority for your charitable budget. Your committee can then either focus on quality of life in other communities where you sell your products or services, or concentrate on recreation and education in your hometown.

## CONDUCTING THE REVIEW-REVISION PROCESS

Figuring out how to do the review and evaluation is still a challenge. Some of the academic and professional resources available were discussed in Chapter 14.

Doing a major revision can be as challenging as starting your program from scratch. Although this book provides you with many of the guidelines you need to get a good framework for your program, when you are in the early stages of program development, you may want to engage an outside consultant to facilitate the process. Over the past half-dozen years, a new breed of financial advisor has moved onto the scene: the philanthropy consultant. In contrast to financial planners, who assist clients in building and preserving net worth, philanthropy consultants are concerned with helping clients to give money away wisely and well, preserving financial control, and sustaining their companies' values.

The Philanthropic Initiative (TPI), a nonprofit group that provides philanthropy consulting and other educational and research services (www.tpi.com), reports that as of 2000, there were some 150 philanthropy consultants across the United States. TPI also admits that more professionals are needed in this field.[1] What is causing this demand for advice in philanthropy?

As far as the business community is concerned, the demand is due to the spectacular growth of the economy and stock market during the 1990s and into the 2000s. Even with the recent downturn in the economy, many older companies have stock that has appreciated dramatically.

Some of this kind of counseling used to be handled by (and still is done with the advice of) the company's attorney and/or accountant. Unfortunately, these persons are not usually trained to do such work, and often find it a misuse of their expensive time.

Accountants may offer advice on appropriate administrative procedures regarding that area of foundation administration and provide accounting and tax services for the new charity. Most accountants are not prepared, however, to address the programmatic framework or grant decision making. In addition, they usually prefer not to be involved in these issues that are so closely tied to the client's intimate family and personal interests and values.

Attorneys may be involved with the mechanics of setting up the paperwork for a family foundation tied to a closely held business, but they seldom are engaged in the planning and decision-making process for grant making.

What do philanthropy consultants do that attorneys and accountants don't? Actually, the field is still in the stage of defining itself, so there is a wide range of what philanthropy consultants do. Most seem to offer two basic services:

1.  Initial assistance in planning the programmatic and administrative structure of philanthropic institutions such as family foundations and corporate giving programs.

2.  Long-term assistance in administration.

The advisors are facilitators who take clients through the steps described in the other chapters of this book.

In addition to guiding your company's team through this planning process, many philanthropy consultants offer administrative services that complement those offered by the attorney, accountant, and financial planner. Depending on the firm, the consultants will do due diligence on requests, screen proposals, perform evaluations, represent donors at recognition functions, issue press releases, and conduct grants meetings, in addition to handling correspondence between trustees, development officers, other advisors, and so on.

Who are these philanthropy consultants? Most of the newcomers to the field (and they are the majority) come out of fundraising. Many have worked in the area of major and planned giving and are familiar with a variety of charitable vehicles for estate planning. They have worked with foundation trustees and with high-net-worth families. Over the years, they have come to recognize the elements required for putting together a rational philanthropic legacy. Because philanthropy consultancy is an emerging field, its members have yet to form an association, but as former fundraisers they adhere to the ethical standards of the Association of Fundraising Professionals (AFP) or the National Committee on Planned Giving (NCPG). The latter claims hundreds of attorneys, accountants, insurance professionals, and financial planners in its ranks.

Some come from the ranks of the wealthy themselves. One of the pioneers in promoting the concept of philanthropy planning is Tracy Gary, a scion of the Pillsbury family.

Others come out of the field of philanthropy. After having served as program officers for one or two private or corporate foundations, they strike out on their own to share what they know with those who need it.

Larger public relations firms may offer philanthropy consulting to their corporate clients. They will do studies and make recommendations on charities for the purpose of cause-related marketing or special promotions. Some philanthropy consulting firms specialize in corporate philanthropy, while offering a broad range of services to businesses and families.

The majority of philanthropy consultants are home-officers, who operate locally or regionally. They offer the distinct advantage of having in-depth knowledge of and contacts with organizations in their areas. For those who provide administration, proximity to the principal trustees and other foundation and estate advisors is vital in maintaining strong personal and professional communications.

Finding a philanthropy consultant is difficult, especially in smaller towns or very large cities. Because of the newness of the field, they cannot advertise in general-interest publications; although some are listed in the *Chronicle of Philanthropy* or in industry publications such as the American Banking Association *Bank Marketing* magazine. Consulting with a local chapter of the National Committee on Planned Giving may yield a contact. Consultants who are aggressive in marketing their services may have spoken before chapter meetings of associations of attorneys, CPAs, or other professionals, and those associations may have information on file.

A company that can benefit from working with a philanthropy consultant will do well to keep looking until it finds one. The expertise they provide can save your company years of fruitless effort and experimentation—time that could have been better spent in effective philanthropy.

## Instituting Change

Once your committee has decided on, approved, and instituted new policies, the members should not keep the information to themselves. Be sure that the changes are communicated to all concerned, especially to the charities with which you work and those you know will come knocking on your door.

Revise all your communications documents to reflect the changes: printed and online guideline statements, applications, brochures, press releases, and the like.

It is of utmost importance for you to communicate changes as soon as possible to charities with which you have a long-term relationship, especially if they would be adversely affected by the changes. If they have come to depend heavily on your company's support, pulling the rug out from under their feet might possibly undo all the good you've done. If your new plan calls for withdrawing future support to an organization, give it a year's notice at the least so that it will have an adequate opportunity to work on finding replacement funding for your contributions.

This is just an extension of the Golden Rule. Certainly, you would not want one of your biggest customers to withdraw its business without giving you ample warning. Don't do the same to a charity!

## COMMUNICATIONS IN GENERAL

When developing a relationship with a charitable partner, good communication is key, just as it is in any good relationship. That communication must start before the relationship begins.

### Guidelines for Grant Seekers

Issuing a set of guidelines for those curious about your giving program will save you and your staff huge amounts of time. When those seeking contributions see this information posted on your website, or read it on a simple postcard, most of them will be deterred from ever going through the application process. There are two reasons for this.

First, many will discover that their program does not fall within your company's criteria for giving: they are outside your geographic area; they do not address your areas of priority, or whatever. Second, if you have a somewhat rigorous application process, many others will refrain because they are simply not willing to put forth the effort.

What should be included in your guidelines?

- Your program's mission statement.
- Grants schedule.
- Areas of priority and what you do *not* fund.
- Grant size limit and nature of grants.
- Contact information for those wishing to proceed with the process.

Make it brief. The information could be formatted to fit on a large postcard, making it very easy for your staff to distribute.

### Notification Letters

Just as you get anxious when waiting for a client's decision about purchasing from you, so do fundraisers wait on pins and needles to hear about the status of their requests.

### Notice of Receipt

To avoid follow-up phone calls from the fundraiser, once the charity has sent in its application, respond with a letter or postcard telling the organization that the application has been received. Give the date of your next contributions committee meeting and inform the group that unless you contact it for additional information, you do not want to hear from it unless there is a major change in the request.

### Decision Notices

Everyone wants to know the good news. When you send a letter notifying a charity that its request has been granted, be sure to tell it the exact amount, the timing of the payment(s), and what you expect from it in return in terms of reporting and recognition.

Of course, no one wants to hear bad news. If you fail to notify a charity that its request has been denied, though, it is inevitable that you will get phone calls, even if your letter of application receipt states that a failure to hear from you after X date meant that the request has been refused. The fundraisers will want to know *why* their applications were refused. So, be sure to tell them in the decision notices the reason why you denied the requests.

## Clarifying Documents

If you are making a grant with strings attached to it, create a short document that describes your conditions. Most fundraisers will have their own drafts prepared for you. In the case of a scholarship bearing your company's name, the draft will probably contain information about the kind of student you want to be the recipient, the areas of study permitted, the grade-point average required, and the like. If you are putting your company's name on a building, the clarifying document will describe the structure and signage. Whatever the fundraiser prepares, don't feel bound to accept it unconditionally. Make sure that your company's interests are honestly and appropriately represented, without tying the hands of the charity should conditions concerning the project change in the future.

## WRAP-UP

Every time you review your corporate citizenship program, refer to the process in this book, starting with your mission and vision, and follow it through to the end. Your initial attempt to develop a program should take about three to five hours, especially if you have an experienced facilitator helping you. Regular revisions will require only an hour or two of the committee's time. By that time, you should have developed enough internal expertise that an outside facilitator will not be needed. Then you can congratulate yourself and your team: You will have graduated from simple good corporate citizens into the class of real corporate philanthropists!

## CHECKLIST

- ❏ Include set review and revision timelines into corporate citizenship policy.
- ❏ Collect and distribute internal and external program evaluation data.
- ❏ Identify changes in company operations or environment that call for program revisions.
- ❏ Revise all communications and documents affected by corporate citizenship program policy changes.
- ❏ Communicate immediately with all concerned parties about changes.
- ❏ Develop guidelines for grant seekers and create standard notification letters.

# PART THREE

# Appendices

# Sample Plans

## High-Tech Corporation
## Corporate Citizenship Plan and Policies

### June 2004

**1.** **Corporate Citizenship Program Mission Statement**

1.1 HIGH-TECH CORPORATION's Corporate Citizenship Program is an effort in which the company and its employees together make a difference in peoples' lives through voluntary service and financial support.

### Internal Guidelines

1.2 The following policies and procedures are meant as guidelines for HIGH-TECH Corporation employees. In keeping with HIGH-TECH's core values, the company wishes to respect the employees' own wisdom and autonomy in guiding this program to reflect the unique abilities of each employee and the equally unique culture and needs of every community where HIGH-TECH has a presence.

**2.** **Decision-Making Bodies for Programs and Grants**

2.1 On a regional level, program and grant decisions will be made by a committee composed of:
- A regional sales or technical services director
- Three (3) volunteers at large

2.1.1 The director does not need to serve as the committee chairperson.

2.1.2 Efforts should be made to maintain geographic and gender diversity on the committee.

2.2 At the headquarters level, program and grant decisions will be made by a committee composed of:
- The Chief Executive Officer
- Three (3) volunteers at large from the headquarters region

2.2.1 Efforts should be made to maintain geographic and gender diversity on the committee.

2.3    Changes to policy will be decided by the Chief Executive Officer and the executive officers of the company.

2.4    *Terms of Service*

2.4.1    The CEO and Regional Directors are permanent members of the committees.

2.4.2    Volunteers at large serve for two-year periods, with terms staggered to allow for citizenship program continuity and consistency.

## 3.    Committee Schedule

3.1    Committees should meet quarterly to review all proposals and requests regarding cash donations and projects that involve employee group participation in volunteer activities.

3.2    Meetings may be in person, by telephone conference call, or by electronic communication.

## 4.    Grants Distributions

4.1    HIGH-TECH Corporation sets a goal of one percent (1%) of pretax profits for distribution as charitable contributions.

4.2    The Executive Committee will make an annual review and decision regarding the division of the 1% between headquarters and regions.

4.3    Funds will be made available for distribution at the regional level in relation to the percent of revenue generated by that region.

4.4    *Limitations*

4.4.1    There is no maximum grant to any organization.

4.4.2    Multiyear grants are allowed.

4.4.3    Automatic renewal of single-year or multiyear grants is allowed.

4.5    *In-kind donations*

4.5.1    In-kind contributions will be allowed, but their value shall not be included toward the goal of one percent (1%).

4.5.2    No limit will be placed on the amount of in-kind contribution, keeping in mind the impact such gifts may have on profits.

4.6    *Employee matching and volunteerism*

4.6.1    HIGH-TECH Corporation encourages employees as individuals to contribute to charities and will match employee gifts to qualified 501(c)(3) charities on a 1:1 basis. The maximum match per employee will be determined annually at the time the annual budget is set. This sum will be included in the giving budget for each region.

4.6.2    Exceptions: Direct contributions to houses of worship or for political activities are not qualified for employee matching gifts.

4.6.3    Individual employees will be allowed 16 hours/year release time for volunteer activities with organizations that relate to priority areas of the HIGH-TECH Corporate Citizenship Program.

4.6.4    HIGH-TECH regional corporate citizenship committees may choose two (2) events per year as official company-sponsored volunteer activities for group participation. Preference should be given to group volunteer activities and events that are proposed to the committee by HIGH-TECH employees.

4.7    *Customer/Partner Requests*

4.7.1   Customers and partners requesting donations for donations or sponsorships must submit an application form to the appropriate HIGH-TECH Corporate Citizenship Committee.

4.7.2   Requests to HIGH-TECH for donations and/or sponsorships for charitable causes will be honored in their relation to the HIGH-TECH Corporate Citizenship Program.

## 5.    Qualified Grant Recipients/Program Focus

5.1     Primary Focus: Most qualified 501(c)(3) organizations, including school districts, are qualified for support. Program grants will be given only for activities and materials that relate to the HIGH-TECH Corporate Citizenship Program priority: INFORMATION TECHNOLOGY.

5.2     Preference will be shown to organizations and projects/programs that address the following:

5.2.1   Information technology equipment and opportunities for disabled/disadvantaged persons.

5.2.2   Institutions that develop information technologies for disabled/disadvantaged persons.

5.2.3   Programs emphasizing youth will be given special consideration.

5.3     Secondary focus: Health. HIGH-TECH recognizes that its corporate social responsibility goes beyond concerned and enlightened self-interest and wishes to extend its resources to problems that confront a broader part of society. HIGH-TECH has an historical relationship with organizations that address health problems. For that reason, proposals and requests for support to organizations associated with those health issues shall also receive priority consideration.

5.4     Disqualified institutions include:

5.4.1   Houses of worship

5.4.2   Political organizations

## 6.    Request Criteria

6.1     Applicants must provide all information and materials requested on the HIGH-TECH Corporation Grant Application Form.

6.2     Applicants must not represent disqualified programs.

## 7.    Communications

7.1     Reporting from grantees

7.1.1   All grantees must provide HIGH-TECH Corporation with an official receipt for any donation.

7.1.2   All grantees must submit a postprogram audit statement highlighting use of HIGH-TECH's grant.

7.1.3   All grantees must provide a written report on the project supported by HIGH-TECH. This can be part of the organization's newsletter or other general publication, such as an annual report, but an individualized report is preferred.

7.2     Recognition from grantees. HIGH-TECH Corporation asks that grantees list HIGH-TECH appropriately as a donor in their official publications and in their other official communication and recognition programs and vehicles.

7.3     Internal and external communications. Communications relating to HIGH-TECH's Corporate Citizenship Program will follow and conform to current communications and public relations policies and procedures.

# High-Tech Corporation
# Corporate Citizenship Program
# Application Information

Date of application: _____

## I.    Organization Background

Organization name: _____

Address: _____

City: _____ State: _____ Zip: _____

Phone: _____ Fax: _____ URL/email: _____

Name and title of person making request: _____

Is the company a HIGH-TECH partner or customer?  Yes _____    No _____

Name and title of chief contact person: _____

Organization's statement of history and purpose: _____

Organization's major accomplishments and capabilities: _____

Name of project for which funds are being sought: _____

## II.    Statement of Need

What problem or issue does your project address?

## III.    Overview of Project

How does your project propose to address the problem? (List objectives and specific tactics.)

_____

_____

If your project is currently under way, what has been accomplished so far?

_____

What unique strength or feature does your organization bring to this problem or issue?

_____

How many staff are committed to this project? _____ How many volunteers? _____

Names of volunteers who are HIGH-TECH employees:

_____

Summarize your action plan and timetable for this project.

_____

_____

How many beneficiaries are targeted by this project?

_____

_____

## IV. Measurable Objectives

What are your short- and long-term goals for this project, and what will be the impact on the target audience?

_____

_____

How will you assess the success or effectiveness of your project? (Give clear, quantifiable objectives to measure the progress of the program.)

_____

_____

## V. Communications Plan

Describe your plan for communicating information about this program to the target audience and the community.

_____

_____

## VI. Relationship to High-Tech Priorities

Describe how this project relates to the priorities of the HIGH-TECH Corporate Citizenship Program.

_____

_____

## VII. Additional Information

Do you belong to any association or consortium? (e.g., United Way) _____

Does your organization sell, rent, loan, exchange, or share your donor list with any other nonprofit or profit-making organizations?  Yes _____   No _____

## VIII. Supporting Documents — Checklist

- ☐ IRS Tax Ruling 501(c)(3) or 509(a)(1).
- ☐ Audited financial statement.
- ☐ Line-item program budget (suggested form attached).
- ☐ List of Board of Directors/Officers and their affiliations.
- ☐ Annual report/Financial statement/Statement of cash flow.
- ☐ If this is a request for a renewal of or increase in a previous grant, list dates when receipts and reports on that grant were sent to HIGH-TECH.
- ☐ Two letters of support from other donors or community leaders.

# Project Budget Worksheet

## Preliminary Projections

| Revenue Source | Amount | Date Requested | Approved |
|---|---|---|---|
| HIGH-TECH Corp. (request) | _____ | _____ | _____ |
| Businesses | | | |
| _____ | _____ | _____ | _____ |
| _____ | _____ | _____ | _____ |
| _____ | _____ | _____ | _____ |
| _____ | _____ | _____ | _____ |
| _____ | _____ | _____ | _____ |
| Foundations | | | |
| _____ | _____ | _____ | _____ |
| _____ | _____ | _____ | _____ |
| _____ | _____ | _____ | _____ |
| _____ | _____ | _____ | _____ |
| _____ | _____ | _____ | _____ |
| Public agencies | | | |
| _____ | _____ | _____ | _____ |
| _____ | _____ | _____ | _____ |
| _____ | _____ | _____ | _____ |
| _____ | _____ | _____ | _____ |
| Individuals (total) | _____ | _____ | _____ |
| Grantee budgeted contribution | _____ | _____ | _____ |
| Other | | | |
| _____ | _____ | _____ | _____ |
| _____ | _____ | _____ | _____ |
| _____ | _____ | _____ | _____ |
| _____ | _____ | _____ | _____ |
| Total | _____ | _____ | _____ |

**Expenses**

Salaries _____

Fringe benefits _____

Interns _____

Consultant fees _____

Conferences/meetings _____

Printing/publications _____

Rent and utilities _____

Telephone _____

Supplies _____

Postage _____

Equipment purchases (list) _____

_____

_____

Total _____

Equipment maintenance _____

Travel _____

Other (list) _____

_____

_____

Total _____

**Total** _____

# Application Evaluation Worksheet

|  | Low | 1 | 2 | 3 | 4 | 5 | High |  |
|---|---|---|---|---|---|---|---|---|
| 1. Is the application complete? | | 1 | 2 | 3 | 4 | 5 | | _____ |
| 2. Are all materials requested included? | | 1 | 2 | 3 | 4 | 5 | | _____ |
| 3. How closely do the project's goals match HIGH-TECH's program priorities? | | 1 | 2 | 3 | 4 | 5 | | _____ |
| 4. How important is HIGH-TECH's grant to the project's overall success? | | 1 | 2 | 3 | 4 | 5 | | _____ |
| 5. Will HIGH-TECH gain publicity, recognition, or growth potential from this project? | | 1 | 2 | 3 | 4 | 5 | | _____ |
| 6. Will this project provide benefits to the maximum number of people possible? | | 1 | 2 | 3 | 4 | 5 | | _____ |
| 7. Are we confident that the organization will respect our rights as donors? | | 1 | 2 | 3 | 4 | 5 | | _____ |
| 8. Are HIGH-TECH employees involved on a volunteer level or was the project proposed by a HIGH-TECH employee? | | 1 | 2 | 3 | 4 | 5 | | _____ |
| 9. Does this project address youth? | | 1 | 2 | 3 | 4 | 5 | | _____ |
| 10. Does this project address health? | | 1 | 2 | 3 | 4 | 5 | | _____ |

**Total** _____

# High-Tech Corporation
# Guidelines for Grant Seekers

## Corporate Citizenship Mission Statement

HIGH-TECH Corporation's Corporate Citizenship Program will be an effort in which its employees can choose to make a difference through service and sharing of knowledge.

## Program Priorities

### Primary Focus:  Information Technology

Preference will be shown to organizations and projects/programs that address the following:

- Information technology equipment and opportunities for disabled/disadvantaged persons, especially children.
- Institutions that develop information technologies for disabled/disadvantaged persons, especially children.

### Secondary Focus:  Health Care

HIGH-TECH has an historical relationship with organizations that address health problems. For those reasons, proposals and requests for support to organizations associated with those health issues shall also receive preferential consideration.

### Qualifying Organizations

Most qualified 501(c)(3) organizations, including school districts, are qualified for support.
HIGH-TECH Corporation does not support:

- Houses of worship
- Political organizations or activities

## Cash/In-Kind Grants and Volunteer Time/Action Requests

### Cash and In-Kind Grants

- There is no maximum grant to any organization.
- Multiyear grants are allowed.
- Automatic renewal of single-year or multiyear grants is allowed.

### Employee Matching and Volunteerism

- HIGH-TECH Corporation encourages employees as individuals to contribute to charities and will endeavor to match employee gifts to qualified 501(c)(3) charities on a 1:1 basis to a maximum determined annually.
- HIGH-TECH employees are allowed 16 hours/year release time for volunteer activities with organizations that relate to priority areas of the HIGH-TECH Corporate Citizenship Program.
- HIGH-TECH regional corporate citizenship committees choose two (2) events per year as official company-sponsored volunteer activities for group participation. Preference is given to group volunteer activities and events that are proposed to the committee by HIGH-TECH employees.

## Customer/Partner Requests

Customers and partners requesting donations or sponsorships must submit an application form to the appropriate HIGH-TECH Corporate Citizenship Committee.

## Sponsorships

Requests to HIGH-TECH for donations and/or sponsorships for charitable causes will be honored if they relate to the HIGH-TECH Corporate Citizenship Program priority areas.

## Applying for a Grant from High-Tech Corporation

- Grants are considered only through the application process.
- Application forms may be obtained by writing to:

> Corporate Citizenship Committee
> HIGH-TECH Corporation
> 123 Technology Circle
> Yourtown, ST 12345

> You may request an application by calling: 1-800-555-TECH
> Applications can be downloaded from HIGH-TECH Corporation's website: *www.hightechcorp.net*

> You may also obtain applications from our regional offices:
> [*list of regional office contact information*]

# Expanding Bank
# Community Involvement Plan and Policies

### June 2004

## 1.    Preamble, Vision, and Mission

1.1    Preamble

Expanding Bank has grown within the communities it has served since 1949. As a member of an interdependent community, Expanding Bank would like to help other community members. This assistance may be in the form of time, talent, or money.

Bank ownership and management believes that individuals and corporations are responsible for finding ways to improve the communities in which they do business. Bank employees are important stakeholders in the Bank and many Bank employees are involved with charitable organizations. The Bank would like to support its employees in their commitments to helping organizations in need. Furthermore, as a leader in the community, the Bank must provide an example in charitable giving. The Bank has established a Community Involvement Plan and Policies.

1.2    Vision

Expanding Bank's Community Involvement Program is committed to fostering a Bank team that is proud and pleased to work for Expanding Bank. The Bank also strives to be a visible and contributing member of the community.

1.3    Mission

Expanding Bank's Community Involvement Program's goal is to help make the communities in which we do business stronger by supporting the charitable organizations and those in need in our market areas.

Programs supported by Expanding Bank's Community Involvement Program should strive to develop integrity, accountability, responsibility, and community growth or strengthen families.

## 2.    Decision Making

2.1    Community Involvement Committees

Each Expanding Bank retail branch and the Operations Center will appoint a Community Involvement Committee. This committee will consist of a retail manager or operations center manager and one or two volunteer representatives from Expanding Bank's staff.

Each retail manager and the operations manager will be a permanent member of the committee. Other members will serve two-year staggered terms. Current members will select new members by appointment or from staff members who volunteer.

2.2    Steering Committee

The steering committee will consist of:
- Expanding Bank's CEO
- Each retail manager and the operations manager from HBO
- The marketing director
- Other individuals chosen by the CEO

2.3    Members are permitted to send proxies to committee meetings if they are not able to attend.

## 3.    Contributions Schedule

3.1    Community Involvement Committees

3.1.1    Community Involvement committees will meet to consider grants of $100 or more. They will meet on the second Monday of each calendar quarter.

3.1.2    Requests for grants of less than $100 may be decided by committees on an ad-hoc basis.

3.2    Steering Committee

The Steering Committee will meet to consider grants of more than $500 and requests from the Community Involvement committees. They will meet on the second Friday of each calendar quarter.

3.3    Location Schedule

Steering Committee meetings will be held at a location chosen by the CEO of Expanding Bank.

## 4.    Grants Distribution

4.1    Expanding Bank intends to contribute two percent (2%) of pretax profits to community organizations. This will be achieved through a combination of cash giving, in-kind giving, and the value of employee volunteer time contributed.

4.2    Employee Matching Gifts

4.2.1    Qualified matches: Expanding Bank's Community Involvement Program will reserve $5,000 from the Steering Committee budget to match donations from employees to any and all qualified 501(c)(3) charities.

4.2.2    Expanding Bank will match contributions on a 1:1 dollar basis up to $50/employee.

4.2.3    Matches will be made for each employee once a year, on a rolling schedule. Employees' annual applications for matching grants may designate a single charity as a recipient of their matching grant.

4.2.4    Requests for matches can be met only if they are made on an official Expanding Bank Community Involvement Program application form.

4.2.5    Available matching funds will not exceed $5,000/year. Requests for matching funds received after the $5,000 allocation has been exhausted will be denied.

4.2.6    Contributions by employees to the Expanding Bank United Way campaign will not be counted toward the $50 annual maximum/employee for matching purposes.

## 5.    Qualified Grant Recipients

5.1    Program Focus

Each grant committee will give highest priority to organizations that promote the development of commerce, especially through program activities and scholarships. Additionally, high priority will be given to programs that support strengthening families.

5.2    Applicants

Preference will be shown to requests submitted to the committees from organizations that are Expanding Bank customers, or individuals who are Expanding Bank customers and who are associated with organizations supporting priority programs.

5.3 Medical/disease-related organizations may receive donations only as a match to an employee gift, or a direct, unmatched gift if the proposal is submitted by an employee who is an active volunteer with the organization or participating in an event to benefit the organization.

5.4 All organizations must have administrative offices and/or program activities located in Expanding Bank's market areas.

5.5 Disqualified Organizations

5.5.1 Houses of worship for activities directly related to religious or worship activities, or for capital construction.

5.5.2 Competitions for community ambassadors/representatives.

## 6. Grant Request Information

6.1 Applicants must provide all information and materials requested on the Expanding Bank Community Involvement Program Grant application form.

6.2 Requests must be received by the due date to be considered for the next grants committee meeting.

6.3 Grant applications will be judged and qualified according to the evaluation criteria listed.

6.4 Applicants must not represent disqualified programs.

## 7. Staff Time Volunteer Plan

Part of the Bank's contribution plan includes volunteer time. The purpose of the volunteer time is to give back to the community and make it stronger and more vibrant. A secondary objective is to allow our staff to get to know each other better and foster a sense of teamwork. To achieve these goals, the Bank has the following guidelines for employee charitable participation during normal work hours.

7.1 The Bank will donate one day of employee time per year per employee to charitable organizations.

7.1.1 This program is voluntary.

7.1.2 Employees need to have prior approval from their managers to donate work time to a charitable cause.

7.1.3 Employees are encouraged to wear their Expanding Bank-labeled clothing at sponsored events.

7.2 The steering committee will identify and sponsor one or more events annually in which employees can participate.

7.2.1 Bank staff will receive their pay for a normal day during the volunteer event.

7.2.2 An Expanding Bank employee will act as the volunteer plan coordinator for each event we sponsor and will oversee all aspects of that event.

## 8. Communication, Recognition, Promotion, and Celebration

8.1 Communication

8.1.1 Internal communication and promotion. Information about the policies and procedures of the Expanding Bank Community Involvement Program will be available in the Expanding Bank Capabilities Book, the internal newsletter, and the intranet announcement system.

8.1.2   External communication and promotion. Forms, guidelines, and other public information about the Expanding Bank Community Involvement Program will be available to program applicants and other interested parties on Expanding Bank's website and in print at Expanding Bank locations and through the mail.

8.2     Recognition

8.2.1   Expanding Bank appreciates recognition from recipient organizations for support given through Community Involvement Program grants.

8.2.2   Expanding Bank requires written reports at least once a year on the specific use of its gift by the recipient organization.

8.3     Internal Celebration

        Expanding Bank will include highlights of the Community Involvement Program in its semiannual employee recognition event.

# Expanding Bank
# Community Involvement Program
# Grant Application Form

Please follow this format. Attach additional sheets of text as necessary. Brochures, flyers, leaflets, and other promotional materials may be appended. Please limit text to a maximum of five (5) pages.

Applications for donations in 2004 are due to Expanding Bank by June 10, September 10, or December 10 to be eligible for consideration at the next quarterly meeting.

## I.    Organization Background

Organization name: _____

Address: _____

City: _____ State: _____ Zip: _____

Phone: _____ Fax: _____ URL/email: _____

Name and title of person making request: _____

Name and title of chief contact person: _____

Is this organization an Expanding Bank customer? Yes _____   No _____

    If yes, please indicate account number _____

Amount of request: $_____

A. Organization's statement of history and purpose: _____

_____

B. Organization's major accomplishments and capabilities: _____

_____

C. Name of project for which funds are being sought: _____

_____

## II.    Statement of Need

How does this project relate to Expanding Bank's Community Involvement Program priorities and mission? (see guidelines)

_____

_____

## III.    Overview of Project

If your project has begun, what has been accomplished so far? _____

_____

What unique strength or feature does your group bring to the community? _____

_____

Please summarize your action plan and timetable for this project. _____

How many beneficiaries are targeted by this project? _____

## IV.  Measurable Objectives

A. What are your short- and long-term goals for this project, and what will be the impact on the target audience?

_____

_____

_____

_____

B. How will you assess the success or effectiveness of your project? (Give clear, quantifiable objectives to measure the progress of the program.)

_____

_____

_____

_____

C. How closely do this project's goals match the Expanding Bank Community Involvement Program mission and guidelines? Explain.

_____

_____

_____

## V.  Communications Plan

Describe your plan for communicating information about this program to the community and individuals who may benefit from your program.

*Grantees must report on the use of funds within six months of receiving the grant. Failure to provide a report, including financial data, will disqualify the grantee from receiving grants from Expanding Bank in the next fiscal year.*

## Supporting Documents Required

- IRS Tax Ruling 501(c)(3) or 509(a)(1)
- Audited financial statement
- Line-item program budget (suggested form attached)
- List of Board of Directors/Officers
- Annual report/Financial statement/Statement of cash flow

# Expanding Bank
## Community Involvement Program Grant
## Project Budget Worksheet

Organization name: _____

Project name: _____

## Preliminary Projections

| Revenue Source | Amount | Date Requested | Approved |
|---|---|---|---|
| Expanding Bank (request) | _____ | _____ | _____ |
| Businesses | | | |
| _____ | _____ | _____ | _____ |
| _____ | _____ | _____ | _____ |
| _____ | _____ | _____ | _____ |
| _____ | _____ | _____ | _____ |
| Foundations | | | |
| _____ | _____ | _____ | _____ |
| _____ | _____ | _____ | _____ |
| _____ | _____ | _____ | _____ |
| _____ | _____ | _____ | _____ |
| Public agencies | | | |
| _____ | _____ | _____ | _____ |
| _____ | _____ | _____ | _____ |
| _____ | _____ | _____ | _____ |
| _____ | _____ | _____ | _____ |
| Individuals (total) | _____ | _____ | _____ |
| Grantee budgeted contribution | _____ | _____ | _____ |
| Other | | | |
| _____ | _____ | _____ | _____ |
| _____ | _____ | _____ | _____ |
| _____ | _____ | _____ | _____ |
| Total | _____ | _____ | _____ |

**Expenses**

Salaries                          _____

Fringe benefits                   _____

Interns                           _____

Consultant fees                   _____

Conferences/meetings              _____

Printing/publications             _____

Rent and utilities                _____

Telephone                         _____

Supplies                          _____

Postage                           _____

Equipment purchase                _____

                                  _____

                                  _____

Equipment maintenance             _____

Travel                            _____

Other (list)                      _____

                                  _____

                                  _____

                                  _____

                                  _____

**Total**                         _____

# Expanding Bank
# Community Involvement Program
# Grant Application Evaluation Worksheet

Organization: _____  Request amt. $ _____

---

## Part 1:  No score

1. Is the application complete?           _____ YES       _____ NO

2. Is the application on time?            _____ YES       _____ NO

3. Are all materials requested included?  _____ YES       _____ NO

## Part 2:  Score 5 for yes, 0 for no

4. Is the organization an Expanding Bank customer, or is the person submitting the request a Bank customer?           _____ YES 5       _____ NO 0

5. Is the person submitting the request an Expanding Bank employee?           _____ YES 5       _____ NO 0

## Part 3:  SCALE    Low   1  2  3  4  5    High

6. How closely do the project's goals match the Expanding Bank Community Involvement Program mission and priorities?

   a.  Strengthen families?                         1  2  3  4  5     _____

   b.  Reach people in need?                        1  2  3  4  5     _____

   c.  Improve someone's ability to begin, grow or improve a commercial enterprise?        1  2  3  4  5     _____

   d.  Develop integrity, accountability, responsibility, community growth?        1  2  3  4  5     _____

   e.  In market area?                               1  2  3  4  5     _____

   f.  Provide visibility?                           1  2  3  4  5     _____

7. How important is Expanding Bank's grant to the project's overall success?           1  2  3  4  5     _____

8. Will this project provide benefits to individuals in need?     1  2  3  4  5     _____

---

**Total**                                                                       _____

---

# Expanding Bank
# Community Involvement Program
# Guidelines for Grant Seekers

## Mission

Expanding Bank's Community Involvement Program's goal is to make our communities stronger by reciprocating the support given to the Bank by our customers and the communities that host us.

Programs supported by Expanding Bank's Community Involvement Program should strive to develop integrity, accountability, responsibility, and community growth or strengthen families.

## Program Priorities

All grants committees will give highest priority to organizations that promote the development of commerce, especially through program activities and scholarships. Programs that support strengthening families will also be given priority.

## Qualified Applicants

All applicants must be current holders of 501(c)(3) charitable status.

Preference will be shown to requests submitted to the committees from organizations that are Expanding Bank customers, or individuals who are Expanding Bank customers and who are closely associated with organizations addressing priority programs.

## Locations

All organizations must have administrative offices and/or program activities located in Expanding Bank's market areas.

## Grant Making

Expanding Bank makes grants of $100 or more four times a year. Grants are approved in January, April, July, and October. Applications are due on the 10th day of December, March, June, and September for consideration at the next quarterly meeting. Requests for gifts of less than $100 are reviewed on a rolling basis.

There is no limit on the size of grants.

## Recognition and Reporting

Expanding Bank appreciates recognition from recipient organizations for support given through Community Involvement Program Committee grants.

Expanding Bank requires written reports at least once a year on the specific use of its support by the recipient organization. *Failure to submit reports, including financial data, will disqualify the grantee from receiving grants from Expanding Bank for the next fiscal year.*

**Applying for a Grant from Expanding Bank Community Involvement Program**

All requests for more than $100 must come in the form of an application following a prescribed format. You may request the application format by calling (888) 555-BANK or writing to:

> Community Involvement Program
> Expanding Bank
> 100 Exbank Way
> Yourtown, ST 12345
> Attn: Carol F.
>
> Applications can be downloaded from the
> Expanding Bank website: *www.exbankinc.com*

Requests for support of less than $100 may be in the form of a letter sent to the local unit of Expanding Bank or to the:

> Expanding Bank Community Involvement Program Steering Committee
> 100 Exbank Way
> Yourtown, ST 12345

# Expanding Bank
# Employee Matching Gifts Program
# Information for Employees

Expanding Bank's Community Involvement Program has reserved $5,000 from the Steering Committee budget to match donations from employees to any and all qualified 501(c)(3) charities. Expanding Bank will match contributions on a 1:1 dollar basis.

- Maximum match is $50/employee.
- Matches will be made to each employee only once a year, on a rolling schedule. Annual applications for matching grants may designate multiple charities as recipients of grants to a total of $50.
- Requests for matches must be made on an official Expanding Bank Community Involvement Program application form.

Available matching funds will not exceed $5,000/year. Requests for matching funds received after the $5,000 allocation has been exhausted will be refused.

***United Way:*** Contributions by employees to the Expanding Bank United Way campaign will not be counted toward the $50 annual maximum/employee for matching purposes unless requested.

## Instructions

Fill out the information in the space provided below. Include the name and address of each charity to receive a matching gift from Expanding Bank, along with a photocopy of the receipt from the donation you wish to have matched. Send the form to the Expanding Bank Community Involvement Program. Your donation may exceed the amount to be matched, but Expanding Bank will match only up to a total of $50 for all your contributions.

Your application will be returned if a grant cannot be funded.

### *Employee Information*

Name: _____

Job title: _____

Expanding Bank unit: _____

Total amount requested (total should not exceed $50): $_____

### *Matching Gift Information*

1. Name of nonprofit: _____

   Address: _____

   _____ Photocopy of receipt attached

   $_____ Amount requested for matching

2. Name of nonprofit: _____

   Address: _____

   _____ Photocopy of receipt attached

   $_____ Amount requested for matching

# Sample Form Letters

## Employee Matching-Gift Letter

Date

Director
Name of Charity
Address
Address

To the Director:

Enclosed please find a check in the amount of $_____ from YOUR COMPANY in support of [*name of charity*]. This donation is made to match the following gifts from YOUR COMPANY employees:

| Name of Employee | Date of donation | $_____ |
|---|---|---|
| Name of Employee | Date of donation | $_____ |
| Name of Employee | Date of donation | $_____ |

We request that you do not include YOUR COMPANY on your mailing list for solicitations and that you do not sell, rent, trade, exchange, or share our name and address with any other charity or business. Should we receive unsolicited correspondence or communication from your organization or other group traceable to your organization as a result of this donation, you will be disqualified from future donations through this program.

Please send a receipt for this donation to my attention at the address on this letterhead.

We wish you continued success in accomplishing your worthy mission.

Sincerely,

Name
Chief Executive Officer

## Missing Information Letter

Date

Name
Charity's Name
Address
Address

Dear Name,

We have received your application for a grant from Company Name. We have given your application an initial review and found that the following information was missing:

_____ Endorsement by Company Name employee

_____ IRS Tax Ruling 501(c)(3) or 509(a)(1)

_____ Audited financial statement

_____ Line-item program budget.

Please submit this information before [*date*] so that we may give your application our full consideration at our next grants meeting. Thank you.

Sincerely,

Name
Chief Executive Officer

## Regret Letter

Date

Name
Charity's Name
Address
Address

Dear Name,

On behalf of the Company Name Charitable Program Committee, I regret to inform you that we are unable to fulfill your request for a grant of $_____ for [*name of project*].

While your project is indeed worthwhile, we receive far more requests than our budget allows. In addition, your request was denied because

    _____ Application/materials were incomplete

    _____ Application was not delivered on time

    _____ Program is outside of Company Name market area

    _____ Program lacked endorsement by Company Name employee

    _____ Program did not match Company Name program priorities well

We wish you the best of luck in attracting other funders to this project. Please feel welcome to reapply to Company Name for another project in the future.

Sincerely,

Name
Chief Executive Officer

## Grant Approval Letter

Date

Director
Name of Charity
Address
Address

To the Director:

On behalf of Company Name, I am pleased to enclose a check in the amount of $_____ in support of [N*ame of Charity/Title of Project*]. Congratulations on presenting such a compelling case.

As indicated in our application form, we expect that you will send us periodic reports on the progress and results of this project, including financial data on the precise us of our funds. Please notify us as soon as possible if there is any change in the way you intend to use our grant. In addition, we request that you send us samples and indications of acknowledgments of our grant, both internal and external to your organization. Representatives of the Company Name Charitable Program Committee will be pleased to visit your facility or attend activities relating to this program. Failure to meet these requirements will disqualify your organization from receiving grants in the future.

Company Name is pleased to be a partner with [*name of charity*] in achieving your mission. We wish you continued success.

Sincerely,

Name
Chief Executive Officer

## Grant Format Information Letter

Date

Name
Name of Charity
Address
Address

Dear Name,

Thank you for your inquiry about the Corporate Citizenship Program at Company Name.

Company Name does not require a proposal or application form from charity groups seeking support. Enclosed please find a set of our Corporate Citizenship Program guidelines to aid you in crafting a letter to us. Your letter should be no longer than three pages, double-spaced. Any additional pages will be discarded and your letter will be evaluated on the basis of the information in the first three. Please do not enclose any brochures or other illustrative materials.

Company Name will inform you immediately when your letter has been received. That notice will also tell you when our committee will meet to consider your request. Please do not contact us after sending your letter unless you do not receive a confirmation of receipt within two weeks or if there is a major change in the program for which you are seeking support. If we have any questions prior to our grants meeting, we will contact you.

We appreciate your interest in having Company Name become your partner in carrying out your organization's mission. Good luck in your fine work.

Sincerely,

Name
Chief Executive Officer

# Press Release

---

**Your Company Letterhead**

---

For immediate release:                              Contact: *Your Name*
Date                                                Telephone: (612) 555-6664

### *Your Company* **Makes Record-Breaking Grant**

*Your Name*, President of *Your Company* Technologies in Yourtown, today announced a record-breaking grant of $1,000,000 to Technology for the Blind. The grant will enable Technology for the Blind, a nonprofit organization headquartered in Golden Valley, to purchase state-of-the-art equipment for its sheltered workshop operation.

"We are proud to support Technology for the Blind in this meaningful way," stated *Your Name*. "Our mission in making grants is to enable disadvantaged groups to have greater access to appropriate technologies. Technology for the Blind provides employment for dozens of blind youth and trains hundreds more to use technology in workplaces in the general market."

Mary Jones, Executive Director of Technology for the Blind, says that this grant will allow them to upgrade equipment that is obsolete. It is the largest grant ever received by Technology for the Blind.

Jones and *Your Name* both credit *Your Company* sales representative Joe Schmoe with starting the process that led to the record-breaking donation. Schmoe, of Yourtown, has been a volunteer with Technology for the Blind since high school.

"Because Joe has been so instrumental in creating this relationship, we have named him *Your Company*'s Volunteer of the Year," announced *Your Name*.

*Your Company* Technologies was founded in 1988. It provides an array of website development and hosting services for business and individuals. For more information about *Your Company*, contact *Your Name* at (612) 555-6664 or refer to *www.yourcompanytech.com*. For more information about Technology for the Blind, contact Mary Jones at (612) 555-4792 or *www.tbusa.org*.

# Sample Scholarship Letters of Agreement

## Preamble

The *Your Company* Award Fund is established at the Technical Institute through a gift(s) from *Your Company*. *Your Company* is a leader in the development and manufacture of widgets for home and industry.

### Nature and Purpose of Fund

The *Your Company* Award Fund is established as a current account, to be distributed annually.

The *Your Company* Award Fund will provide $2,500 for one student per year and the award for that student is not renewable.

### Selection and Qualification

The *Your Company* Award will be conferred upon a student who has demonstrated exceptional talent in Widget Science. Should winners of the *Your Company* Award be eligible for financial aid, the award should not reduce the amount of their funds-in-aid. The *Your Company* Award may be used to underwrite the winner's tuition and fees and/or travel expenses, registration fees, and associated costs for attending Widget Society conferences and conventions and other supplementary activities to Widget Studies.

Selection shall be made by a committee of the Widget Science faculty at Technical Institute and (after the first *Your Company* Award winner graduates) a past *Your Company* Award winner, if possible.

### Additional Benefits to Winner

Winners of the *Your Company* Award are eligible for a paid internship in the Widget Research and Development Division of *Your Company* the year following the award, conditional upon the student achieving a 3.8 or higher in Widget Science classes.

## Communication and Recognition

*Your Company* shall receive a report, written or in person, from Technical Institute on the academic progress of each of the *Your Company* Award Scholars on an annual basis.

Students (and their parents, if possible) shall be notified that the student is the recipient of the *Your Company* Award. *Your Company* welcomes communications in writing or in person from the student.

*Your Company* may be listed on all Technical Institute honor rolls and in appropriate publicity.

## Contingency

If, in the future, circumstances arise making it unwise or unnecessary in the opinion of the Technical Institute Board of Directors to use the funds for the purpose specified above, then the Directors may, in their discretion and, when possible, in consultation with *Your Company,* use the funds for the fulfillment of the objectives set forth, maintaining its named identity if possible.

*Signed*

_____                    _____

Technical Institute President                       *Your Company* CEO
[DATE]

# Jane Roe Memorial Scholarship Fund

## Preamble

The Jane Roe Scholarship Fund is established through a gift from *Your Company* in memory of its late CEO, Jane Roe. Jane Roe was one of the original students at Community College, an exceptionally creative talent who worked for her entire career with *Your Company,* rising from a position in computer animation to the company's highest position.

## Nature and Purpose of Fund

The Jane Roe Memorial Scholarship Fund is established as an endowment, to be distributed annually to a student at Community College.

The Jane Roe Memorial Scholarship Fund will provide up to one-half of the cost of tuition for at least one student per year who is eligible for financial aid. The award is renewable, contingent upon the student(s) maintaining a 2.8 average.

## Selection and Qualification

Eligible Jane Roe Scholars will be selected from existing students at Community College.

Selection shall be made by the Community College Scholarship Committee and an employee of *Your Company* who is also a graduate of Community College, if possible.

*Your Company* shall receive a report, written or in person, on the progress of each of the Jane Roe Scholars on an annual basis.

## Recognition and Acknowledgment

*Your Company* may be acknowledged in Community College publications and other honor rolls.

## Contingency

If, in the future, circumstances arise making it unwise or unnecessary in the opinion of the Community College Board of Directors to use the funds for the purpose specified above, then the Directors may, in their discretion and if possible in consultation with *Your Company,* use the funds for the fulfillment of the objectives set forth, maintaining its named identity if possible.

*Signed*

_____          _____
Community College President              Name, *Your Company* CEO
[DATE]                                    [DATE]

# Jill Moe Scholarship Fund

## Preamble

The Jill Moe Scholarship Fund is established at the Private Arts School through a gift(s) from *Your Company* in honor of our CEO, Jill Moe, upon her retirement. Jill Moe is a long-time resident of Yourtown, a product of the Private Arts School system, and the parent of a graduate of the Private Arts School.

## Nature and Purpose of Fund

The Jill Moe Scholarship Fund is established as a quasi-endowment, to be distributed annually. Should interest be insufficient in any given year to provide adequate support for the purpose described below, then the Private Arts School Directors are permitted to invade the principal. This shall not be allowed to occur more than once per ten-year period.

The Jill Moe Scholarship Fund will provide up to one-half of the cost of tuition for at least one student per year who is eligible for tuition reduction. The award is not renewable and should be used for recruitment purposes only.

## Selection and Qualification

Eligible Jill Moe Scholars will be selected from candidates from within the City of Yourtown, and preferably from within the Centercity neighborhood. Students must come from families eligible for tuition reduction. The Jill Moe Scholarship should form the complete tuition reduction package for that student.

Selection shall be made by the Tuition Reduction Committee with approval from a member of the *Your Company* executive management committee.

Students and parents shall be notified that the student is the recipient of the Jill Moe Scholarship, funded by *Your Company. Your Company* welcomes communications in writing or in person from the student and/or the family.

*Your Company* may be listed on all Private Arts School honor rolls and in appropriate publicity.

## Contingency

If, in the future, circumstances arise making it unwise or unnecessary in the opinion of the Private Arts School Board of Directors to use the funds for the purpose specified above, then the Directors may, in their discretion and if possible in consultation with *Your Company,* use the funds for the fulfillment of the objectives set forth, maintaining its named identity and recognition of *Your Company* if possible.

*Signed*

_____

Private Arts School
Principal
[DATE]

_____

Name
*Your Company* CEO

# Selected Resources for Corporate Citizenship Planning and Education

**American Society for Quality** 600 N. Plankinton Ave., Milwaukee, WI, 53203, (800) 248-1946, *www.asq.org*. A membership organization for business, government, education, and nonprofit institutions dedicated to achievement of total quality management, including corporate citizenship. This group administers the prestigious Baldrige Awards program.

**Austin Entrepreneurs Foundation** PO Box 684826, Austin, TX, 78768-4826, (512) 482-8894. One of the original venture philanthropy funds, their program can be used as a model for others considering entry into this forum for philanthropy.

**Better Business Bureau Wise Giving Alliance** 4200 Wilson Blvd., Suite 800, Arlington, VA, 22203, (703) 276-0100, *www.give.org*. This is a service that reports for individuals and institutions that have made inquiries about charities making solicitations. Charities are evaluated according to the voluntary standards established by the Better Business Bureau for charities.

**Business for Social Responsibility** 111 Sutter St., 12th Floor, San Francisco, CA, 93104, (415) 984-3200, *www.bsr.org*. BSR is a global organization formed to help its member companies to integrate respect for their communities, their people, and the environment into a formula for business success. In addition to print and on-line information, BSR offers advisory services.

**Caux Round Table, U.S.A**. 401 N. Robert St., St. Paul, MN 55101, (651) 265-2761, *www.cauxroundtable.org*. The Caux Round Table (CRT) is a group of senior business leaders from Europe, Japan, and North America who are committed to the promotion of principled business leadership. Their philosophy is that business has a crucial role in identifying and promoting sustainable and equitable solutions to important issues affecting the world's physical, social, and economic environments. The CRT offers meetings, papers, and commentaries, newletters, tools, and training materials for ethical business conduct.

**Center for Corporate Citizenship at Boston College** W.E. Carroll School of Management, 55 Lee Rd., Chestnut Hill, MA, 02467, (616) 552-8680, *www.bc.edu/bc_org/avp/csom/*

*ccc/index.html*. A research institute that provides standards, tools, executive training, and consulting for bigger businesses as well as statistical reports.

**Center for Ethical Business Cultures** 1000 LaSalle Avenue, MJH 300, Minneapolis, MN, 55403-2005, (651) 962-4120, *www.cebcglobal.org*. CEBC is a partnership between the University of St. Thomas College of Business and the University of Minnesota Carlson School of Management. It aims to build awareness, generate products and services, and educate business leaders present and future in three areas: Ethical leadership, management, and culture; work-life and critical employer-employee relationships; and corporate citizenship.

**Chronicle of Philanthropy** 1255 23rd St. NW, Washington, DC, 20037, (202) 466-1200, *www.philanthropy.com*. A newspaper containing stories and announcements about charities and individual, foundation, and corporate donors. Very useful to beginners in corporate citizenship who want to see what others are doing in the field of philanthropy.

**Committee to Encourage Corporate Philanthropy** 110 Wall St., Suite 2-1, New York, NY 10005, (212) 825-1000, *www.corphilanthropy.org*. Founded by actor and entrepreneur Paul Newman, this group is composed exclusively of CEOs and chairs of large multi-national corporations. They aim to raise awareness among all parts of the business community of the importance of good corporate citizenship and to advocate for legislation to enable it. One aspect of their program available to all is a set of measures and standards for good corporate philanthropy.

**Contributions Academy** 1150 Hungryneck Blvd., Suite C-344, Mount Pleasant, SC, 29464, (843) 216-3443, *www.contributionsacademy.com*. This private firm offers seminars, events, books, speakers, and web conferencing aimed at business managers who work in the areas of contributions, community relations, public affairs, and employee volunteer programs.

**Council on Foundations** 1828 L Street, Washington, DC 20036, (202) 466-6512, *www.cof.org*. Founded in 1949, this is the oldest membership organization in the country for trustees of private and corporate foundations. The Council offers members a vast variety of services from its staff and provides opportunities for trustees to interact and learn from each other. It has a strong research arm and is a leader in legislative advocacy for the nonprofit sector. The Council also sponsors an awards program to honor excellence in professional philanthropy.

**The Philanthropic Initiative** 77 Franklin Street, Boston, MA, 02110, (617) 338-2590, *www. tpi.org*. This nonprofit consulting firm evolved out of a program at Harvard University. TPI provides seminars and publications to complement their research activities.

# Bibliography

American Association of Fundraising Counsel Trust for Philanthropy. *Giving USA 2002: The Annual Report on Philanthropy for the Year 2002.* Bloomington, IN: Center for Philanthropy at Indiana University, 2002.

Americans for the Arts. *Arts and Economic Prosperity: The Economic Impact of Nonprofit Arts Organizations and Their Audiences.* Washington, DC: Americans for the Arts, 2002.

America's Charities and The Consulting Network. *Employee Workplace Campaigns at the Crossroads.* Chantilly, VA: America's Charities and The Consulting Network, 2000.

Blum, Debra. "Teenagers Prefer Companies That Give, Survey Finds." *Chronicle of Philanthropy,* vol. 12, no. 22 (September 7, 2000): 35.

Brandt, Steve. "Minneapolis Sues North Side Nonprofit Alleging Negligence, Fraud." *Star Tribune* [Minneapolis, MN], July 15, 2003, p. 1B.

Cone, Carol L., Mark A. Feldman, and Alison T. DaSilva. "Causes and Effects." *Harvard Business Review,* vol. 81, no. 7 (2003): 95.

Franklin, Robert. "Sports and Charity: High Visibility, Low Bucks." *Star Tribune* [Minneapolis, MN], July 14, 2003, p. 1A.

GVA Marquette Advisors and Maxfield Research, Inc. *Workforce Housing: The Key to Ongoing Regional Prosperity, Executive Summary.* Report for Family Housing Fund. Minneapolis, MN: GVA Marquette Advisors and Maxfield Research, Inc., September 2001.

Hall, Holly. "Equal Sights." *Chronicle of Philanthropy,* vol. 10, no. 14 (May 7, 1998): 15.

Independent Sector. *Giving and Volunteering in the United States: Executive Summary.* New York: Independent Sector, 1999.

Letts, Christine, William Ryan, and Allen Grossman. "Virtuous Capital: What Foundations Can Learn from Venture Philanthropists." *Harvard Business Review,* vol. 75, no. 2 (March–April 1997).

Lockyer, Bill. *Summary of Results of Solicitation by Commercial Fundraisers.* Sacramento, CA: Office of the California Attorney General, 2002.

Mann, Bill. "Buffett Kills Berkshire Charities." *The Motley Fool,* available at *www.Fool.com/news/mft/2003/mft03070702.htm.*

Minneapolis Regional Chamber of Commerce. *Keystone Participant Directory 2002*. Minneapolis, MN: Minnesota Keystone Program, 2002.

O'Connell, Brian. *Civil Society: The Under-pinnings of American Democracy*. Hanover, NH: University Press of New England, 1999.

Paprocki, Steve. *Mergers: Implications for Corporate Philanthropy and the Community*. Minneapolis, MN: Center for Ethical Business Cultures, 2000.

Porter, Michael E., and Mark R. Kramer. "The Competitive Advantage of Corporate Philanthropy." *Harvard Business Review*, vol. 19, no. 2 (December 2002): 61.

Reis, Jackie. *The Business of Giving Back: 2002 Survey of Business Giving and Community Involvement*. Minneapolis, MN: Building Business Investment in Community, 2002.

Rubenstein, Doris. "Bridge the Philanthropy Gap." *CityBusiness: The Business Journal*, vol. 19, no. 21 (October 26, 2001): 62.

Rubenstein, Doris. "Cultural, Historic, and Structural Elements of Leadership in Hispanic Nonprofit Organizations in Minnesota." Master's thesis, Augsburg College, Minneapolis, MN, 1993.

Rubenstein, Doris. "Invest in Reputation Insurance." *CityBusiness: The Business Journal*, vol. 18, no. 48 (April 27, 2001): 60.

Sinclair, Michelle, and Joseph Galaskiewicz. "Corporate-Nonprofit Partnerships: Varieties and Covariates." *New York Law School Law Review*, vol. 41, nos. 3–4 (1997): 1059.

Taylor, Paul. *Industry Analysis Quarterly Survey*. McLean, VA: National Automobile Dealers Association, Spring 2002.

Vidal, David J. *Consumer Expectations on the Social Accountability of Business*. New York: Conference Board, September 1999.

Walker Information, Council on Foundations. *Measuring the Business Value of Corporate Philanthropy: Research Report Executive Summary*. Washington, DC: Council on Foundations, October 2000.

Wolverton, Brad. "No More Wiggle Room." *Chronicle of Philanthropy*, vol. 15, no. 10 (March 6, 2003): 7.

Women's Philanthropy Institute. "Facts About Women, Wealth, and Giving." Available at *www.women-philanthropy.org*.

# Notes

## CHAPTER 1

1. Brian O'Connell, *Civil Society: The Under-pinnings of American Democracy* (Hanover, NH: University Press of New England, 1999): 73.
2. Michael E. Porter and Mark R. Kramer, "The Competitive Advantage of Corporate Philanthropy," *Harvard Business Review,* vol. 19, no. 12 (December 2002): 61.
3. Ibid., p. 7.

## CHAPTER 2

1. David Vidal, *Consumer Expectations on the Social Accountability of Business* [report] (New York: Conference Board, September 1999).
2. The Consulting Network, *Employee Workplace Campaigns at the Crossroads: Recommendations for Revitalization* [Special Report, America's Charities] (Chantilly, VA: Consulting Network, 2000).
3. Walker Information, *Measuring the Business Value of Corporate Philanthropy: Research Report Executive Summary* [Report for the Council on Foundations] (Washington, DC: Walker Information, October 2000).
4. Doris Rubenstein, "Invest in Reputation Insurance," *CityBusiness: The Business Journal*, vol. 18, no. 48 (April 27, 2001): 60.
5. *Business Week* online, September 11, 2000: *www.businessweek.com/2000/00_37/b33698004.htm* (accessed November 11, 2003).
6. Vidal, *Consumer Expectations.*
7. Steve Paprocki, *Mergers: Implications for Corporate Philanthropy and the Community* [report] (Minneapolis, MN: Center for Ethical Business Cultures, 2000).

## CHAPTER 3

1. Jackie Reis, *The Business of Giving Back* [report] (Minneapolis, MN: Building Business Investment in Community, 2002): 5.
2. Doris Rubenstein, "Bridge the Philanthropy Gap," *CityBusiness: The Business Journal,* vol. 19, no. 21 (October 26, 2001): 62.

3. Holly Hall, "Equal Sights," *Chronicle of Philanthropy,* vol. 10, no. 14 (May 7, 1998): 15.

4. Independent Sector, *Giving and Volunteering in the United States: Executive Summary* [report] (New York: Independent Sector, 1999).

5. Brad Wolverton, "No More Wiggle Room," *Chronicle of Philanthropy,* vol. 15, no. 10 (March 6, 2003): 7.

6. Americans for the Arts, *Arts & Economic Prosperity: The Economic Impact of Nonprofit Arts Organizations and Their Audiences* [report] (Washington, DC: Americans for the Arts, 2002), 5.

7. Reis, *The Business of Giving Back,* 5.

## CHAPTER 5

1. Walker Information, *Measuring the Business Value of Corporate Philanthropy.* Published by the Council on Foundations: *www.measuringphilanthropy.com/docs/summary.pdf* (accessed November 11, 2003).

## CHAPTER 7

1. Minneapolis Regional Chamber of Commerce, *Keystone Participant Directory 2002* [report for Keystone Program] (Minneapolis, MN: Minneapolis Regional Chamber of Commerce, 2002): 7.

## CHAPTER 8

1. Debra Blum, "Teenagers Prefer Companies That Give, Survey Finds," *Chronicle of Philanthropy,* vol. 12, no. 22 (September 7, 2000): 35.

## CHAPTER 9

1. Scholarship America was formerly called the Citizen's Scholarship Foundation of America.

2. *www.morino.org/about_vision_foun.asp* (accessed November 15, 2003).

3. *www.efbayarea.org/EF_Brochure_.pdf* (accessed 11/15/03).

4. Community Wealth Ventures, "Venture Philanthropy 2002: Advancing Nonprofit Performance through High-Engagement Grantmaking," Venture Philanthropy Partners, *www.vppartners.org/learning/reports/report2002/report2002.html* (accessed November 15, 2003).

5. "1999 Report on Socially Responsible Investing Trends in the United States," *www.socialinvest.org/areas/research/trends/1999-Trends.htm* (accessed November 15, 2003).

6. Paul Taylor, *Industry Analysis Quarterly Survey* (McLean, VA: National Automobile Dealers Association, Spring 2002).

7. Luchina Fisher, "Women Are Giving Away More Money Than Ever, *www.womensenews.com/article.cfm/dyn/aid/1313* (accessed November 15, 2003).

## CHAPTER 10

1. GVA Marquette Advisors and Maxfield Research, Inc., *Workforce Housing: The Key to Ongoing Regional Prosperity, Executive Summary* [report for Family Housing Fund] (Minneapolis, MN: GVA Marquette Advisors and Maxfield Research, Inc., September 2001): 3.

2. American Association of Fundraising Counsel Trust for Philanthropy, *Giving USA 2002: The Annual Report on Philanthropy for the Year 2002* [report for The Center on Philanthropy at Indiana University] (Bloomington, IN: AAFRC, 2002).

## CHAPTER 11

1. Michelle Sinclair and Joseph Galaskiewicz, "Corporate-Nonprofit Partnerships: Varieties and Co-variates," *New York Law School Law Review,* vol. 41, nos. 3–4 (1997): 1059.

## CHAPTER 12

1. Doris Rubenstein, "Cultural, Historic, and Structural Elements of Leadership in Hispanic Nonprofit Organizations in Minnesota" Master's thesis, Augsburg College, Minneapolis, MN (1993), p. 30.
2. Steve Brandt, "Minneapolis Sues North Side Nonprofit Alleging Negligence, Fraud," *Star Tribune* (Minneapolis) 23, no. 102 (July 15, 2003): 81.
3. Bill Lockyer [Attorney General], "Summary of Results of Solicitation by Commercial Fundraisers" [report for California Attorney General's Office], Sacramento, CA, p. 3, *http//: www.caag.state.ca.us/charities/publications/cfrreport.pdf* (accessed December 8, 2003).

## CHAPTER 14

1. National Institute of Standards and Technology *www.nist.gov/public_affairs/update/upd20030514.htm#Quality* (viewed November 15, 2003).
2. Committee to Encourage Corporate Philanthropy, "Building the Measures," *www.givingstandard.com* (viewed November 15, 2003).

## CHAPTER 15

1. Bill Mann, "Buffett Kills Berkshire Charities," *The Motley Fool, www.fool.com/news/mft/2003/mft 03070703.htm* (July 7, 2003).
2. Carol L. Cone, Mark A. Feldman, and Alison T. DaSilva, "Causes and Effects," *Harvard Business Review* 81, no. 7 (2003): 95.
3. Robert Franklin, "Sports and Charity: High Visibility, Low Bucks," *Star Tribune* (Minnesota) 19, no. 101 (July 14, 2003): A1.

## CHAPTER 16

1. Steve Johnson, "What's a Donor to Do? The State of Donor Resources in America Today" [report]. Boston, MA: The Philanthropic Initiative, November 6, 2000, p. 33.

# Index